Easy Linux Commands
Working Examples of Linux Command Syntax

Easy Linux Series

Jon Emmons
Terry Clark

This book is dedicated to Kirsten for all the weekends we lost to it. Thank you for everything.

Jon Emmons

Easy Linux Commands
Working Examples of Linux Command Syntax

By Jon Emmons & Terry Clark

Copyright © 2006 by Rampant TechPress. All rights reserved.

Printed in the United States of America.

Published in Kittrell, North Carolina, USA.

Easy Linux Series: Book #1

Series Editor: Donald K. Burleson

Editors: Janet Burleson, John Lavender, and Robin Haden

Production Editor: Teri Wade

Cover Design: Janet Burleson

Printing History: October 2006 for First Edition

ISBN: 0-9759135-0-6

Library of Congress Control Number: 2005901265

Table of Contents

CHAPTER 2 - Important Files and Directories

CHAPTER 3 - File and Directory Security

CHAPTER 4 - Linux Search Tools

CHAPTER 5 - The vi Editor

CHAPTER 6 - Shell Scripts

CHAPTER 7 - Scheduling Jobs with crontab

CHAPTER 8 - Linux Administrator Commands

CHAPTER 9 - Monitoring Memory and Processor

CHAPTER 10 - Disk and Filesystem Commands

Using the Online Code Depot

Purchase of this book provides complete access to the online code depot that contains the sample code scripts. All of the code depot scripts in this book are available for download in zip format, ready to load and use and are located at the following URL:

rampant.cc/linux_commands.htm

If technical assistance is needed with downloading or accessing the scripts, please contact Rampant TechPress at info@rampant.cc.

Don't forget to download your Poster!

Your purchase entitles you to the quick reference poster for Linux, an easy way to quickly issue all of the most important Linux commands. Instructions will be in the code depot for the book.

Conventions Used in this Book

It is critical for any technical publication to follow rigorous standards and employ consistent punctuation conventions to make the text easy to read.

However, this is not an easy task. Within Linux there are many types of notation that can confuse a reader. It is also important to remember that many Linux commands are case sensitive, and are always left in their original executable form, and never altered with italics or capitalization.

Parameters - All Linux commands, arguments and parameters will be **bold.**

Variables – All program variables and arguments will also remain in *italics.*

Command Line Sessions – Command line sessions will be represented in a grey box. Commands which the user would type are in **bold** and script output remains un-bolded. The dollar ($) and pound (#) at the beginning of a command typically represent a prompt and should not be typed unless presented in bold.

Programs & Products – All products and programs that are known to the author are capitalized according to the vendor specifications (IBM, DBXray, etc). All names known by Rampant TechPress to be trademark names appear in this text as initial caps. References to UNIX are always made in uppercase.

Acknowledgements

This type of highly technical reference book requires the dedicated efforts of many people. Even though we are the authors, our work ends when we deliver the content. After each chapter is delivered, several Linux experts carefully review and correct the technical content. After the technical review, experienced copy editors polish the grammar and syntax.

The finished work is then reviewed as page proofs and turned over to the production manager, who arranges the creation of the online code depot and manages the cover art, printing distribution, and warehousing.

In short, the authors play a small role in the development of this book, and we need to thank and acknowledge everyone who helped bring this book to fruition:

Janet Burleson, for her production management, including the coordination of the cover art, page proofing, printing, and distribution.

Robin Haden, for her help in the production of the page proofs.

John Lavender, for his assistance with the web site, and for creating the code depot and the online shopping cart for this book.

Jennifer Adkins, for her help with sales and distribution.

Thanks to all the people at Rampant who were involved in the process of completing this book. It could never have happened this way without you.

Many thanks,

Jon Emmons & Terry Clark

Preface

In the past decade Linux has gained a strong foothold in both the server and desktop market. While many common Linux tasks can now be done through a graphical interface, if you use Linux frequently sooner or later there will be a time when the graphical interface will not work or you need to do something remotely and can only get a command-line connection. When that happens it's handy to have a quick reference around. This book is that reference.

Linux was once the exclusive domain of alpha-geeks who thought nothing of compiling their own operating system. However, over the past decade Linux has become a viable, even prominent operating system for everything from large clustered computers to desktops to DVD video players. There are almost as many different distributions of Linux as there are uses and each has its own intricacies. Since distributions are actively developed by loosely knit groups of developers it is impossible to touch on all the features and intricacies of every distribution. The commands in this book will work in most distributions but the documentation for your distribution should be considered the definitive source for more specific information.

As your comfort with the Linux command line increases you will find that some things are easier to do on the command line than they are in a graphical interface. Additionally it is easy to combined Linux commands into shell scripts to perform multiple complex tasks with a single script saving you time and reducing the chances that you forget or mis-type part of the command.

While mastery of the Linux environment can only come with experience and time by including the most popular commands and options in this book we hope to ease the learning curve while providing a reference which will help users at all levels of experience.

Well, if you're ready, let's get started.

Some Important Background Information

We don't want to bore you with a history lesson, but a little background on Linux can help you understand how it works. Don't worry, we'll keep it brief.

What is Linux?

Linux is an operating system loosely based on UNIX, a popular mainframe operating system which was originally developed in the 1960s by AT&T's Bell Laboratories. This is why Linux is often referred to as a "UNIX-like" operating system.

Just like Microsoft Windows, Linux controls the computer hardware, does it's best to keep all your devices playing nicely together and gives you an interface to run things on the computer. Unlike Microsoft Windows there are several groups (some commercial, some non-profit) who make Linux operating systems.

The Linux kernel

The heart of a Linux system is a program called the kernel. The kernel controls security, processors, memory, disk and everything else about the system.

The kernel is what allows multiple users to be on a Linux system at the same time running dozens, possibly even thousands of things at once without interfering with each other. While we won't talk too much more about the kernel, it's just important to remember that it's there keeping everything in check.

The Many Breeds of Linux

You may have already noticed that there are a ton of different Linux versions out there. Many meet only a very specific need while others compete in the mass market for servers and workstations. Here are a couple of the Linux distributions which are popular right now:

Red Hat Enterprise Linux

www.redhat.com/rhel/ - This is the commercial version of Linux used for the examples in this book. It is a popular option for both servers and workstations because it is both feature-rich and well supported.

Fedora

www.redhat.com/fedora/ - Sponsored by Red Hat, this community supported version of Linux is available for free. The free price tag makes this a great version to work with if you don't have (or want to pay for) a license for Red Hat Enterprise Linux, but be careful, some applications which are Red Hat compatible may not work on Fedora.

Ubuntu

www.ubuntu.com - Ubuntu is a Linux-based operating system which has recently gained some popularity. It is easy to install and the desktop version comes with many of the applications you would want on your workstation.

Mileage May Vary

Because no two distributions are quite the same you may find that some commands and options may not work, or may not work as described on your variety of Linux. The examples in this book were done on RedHat Linux. Almost all will work on most flavors of Linux but even a different version of RedHat will vary some.

Installation of Linux varies from distribution to distribution. If you do not already have a Linux system to work on you may want to download one of the versions mentioned above and install it on a spare machine. Unless you are experienced at installing Linux I suggest you choose a machine you will not use for anything else. It is quite possible (even easy) to erase your entire hard drive while installing Linux, so take an old system (it doesn't have to be too fast) that you don't need any of the data on and follow the instructions that come with your distribution to install Linux.

What is a shell?

All the commands we run in this book are run in a Linux shell. A shell in Linux is the software which allows you, a human, interact with the inner workings of the UNIX operating system. Because of the shell we get to use commands that resemble our natural language (though sometimes only just barely) to control the behavior of the computer. There are other types of shells in computing, but this is the only type we're concerned with for this book.

Beyond the ability to use somewhat intuitive commands individually, the shell also gives us the ability to combine these commands into shell scripts. A shell script can contain one command or hundreds and the commands could be nearly anything you could do from within the shell.

The bash shell

There are, of course, many kinds of shells. Each has its strengths and weaknesses but we're mostly concerned with the Bourne-Again Shell (**bash**) which is the default for users in Linux.

If you think your shell may not be **bash** don't worry. We'll talk about how to change it later, but for now you can change it temporarily simply by typing **bash**.

Getting to the shell

You can access a Linux shell in several different ways. You may access the shell by sitting at a Linux computer where the shell is displayed on screen or you may use a secure protocol to enter a shell on a system thousands of miles away.

In some environments you may use a telnet client or, more likely a secure *ssh* client to connect to a Linux machine. This will depend largely on how you your machine and your environment is set up. If you are connecting remotely through one of these clients you should talk with the person who set the machine up to find out how to connect.

Once you're at the Linux command line almost everything works the same whether you're at the keyboard of the system you work on or at a workstation half way around the world.

A few quick tips

Here are a few things that it might help you to know from the beginning. They may seem out of place here, but will make more sense as we get into using Linux.

No news is good news

One thing you will have to get used to is that when you run many common Linux commands if things go right you will not get any feedback. There are very few Linux commands which will tell you "Operation completed successfully." More likely they will tell you nothing *unless* something goes wrong. So basically don't worry if you don't get any feedback from Linux. It'll give you an error if there's a problem.

Tab completion

One feature of the bash shell that we will be using is the ability to complete partially typed commands and file names with the **tab** key. If you type in enough of the command or file to uniquely identify what you're looking for, then press **tab** Linux will complete the file or command. Try it out once we get started. It can save you a lot of typing.

Repeating recent commands with the up arrow

If you want to repeat a recently executed command, or even repeat it with a slight modification, the bash shell will allow you to recall it using the **up arrow**. The **up** and **down arrows** will allow you to go back and forth through your recently typed commands to recall them for execution. This can be very useful if you make a typo and don't want to retype the entire command again.

Getting More Help

While we will cover a lot of ground in this book you may find topics here which you want to learn more about. Linux provides a couple resources available right at the command line to give you more information on commands.

Man Pages

Whenever detailed help is needed with command syntax or with command options, the manual (**man**) command can be used to display all of the information about the specified command. The information will be displayed one screen at a time. Pressing the space bar will advance the next screen. At the end of the display, the **Q** command can be used to quit.

The **man** command should be followed by the name of the command with which help is needed, as shown in the following example:

```
$ man w

W(1)                      Linux User's Manual                      W(1)

NAME
      w - Show who is logged on and what they are doing.

SYNOPSIS
      w - [husfV] [user]

DESCRIPTION
      w  displays  information  about the users currently on the machine, and
      their processes.  The header shows, in this order,  the  current  time,
      how  long  the  system  has  been running, how many users are currently
      logged on, and the system load averages for the past 1, 5, and 15  min-
      utes.

      The  following entries are displayed for each user: login name, the tty
      name, the remote host, login time, idle time, JCPU, PCPU, and the  com-
      mand line of their current process.

      The  JCPU  time  is the time used by all processes attached to the tty.
      It does not include past background jobs, but  does  include  currently
      running background jobs.

      The  PCPU  time  is  the time used by the current process, named in the
      "what" field.

COMMAND-LINE OPTIONS
      -h   Don't print the header.

      -u   Ignores the username while figuring out the  current  process  and
           cpu  times.  To demonstrate this, do a "su" and do a "w" and a "w
           -u".

      -s   Use the short format.  Don't print the login time,  JCPU  or  PCPU
           times.

      -f   Toggle  printing the from (remote hostname) field.  The default as
           released is for the from field to not be  printed,  although  your
           system administrator or distribution maintainer may have compiled
           a version in which the from field is shown by default.

      -V   Display version information.

      user Show information about the specified user only.

FILES
      /etc/utmp
            information about who is currently logged on

      /proc  process information
```

The **man** pages can be a bit confusing but they will often contain
options which are not covered in this book. Be careful when using a
new option for any command.

Info

In situations where users are unsure which command should be used
for a particular function, the **info** command can be used. The info
subsystem contains information about all of the commands and
utilities available within the system. The info system even gives tips for

navigating within the info subsystem. The **info** command is entered to simply invoke the info subsystem.

The info subsystem even offers the capability of entering information about any commands, scripts, etc. for documentation purposes.

Conclusions

In this chapter we discussed what Linux is, why the kernel is so important, and touched on some of the popular varieties of Linux currently available. We then talked about the shell and more specifically about the bash shell which we will be using in this book.

We spent some time setting some expectations of what the shell is going to do for us and discussed some of the usability features that make bash nicer to use.

Though you will be able to use many commands straight out of this book you may find you need more information on certain commands. We showed how the **man** and **info** commands can be used to find out about options and commands that we won't have the time or paper to cover in this book.

Now let's get right into using Linux with some directory and file commands.

Directory and File Commands

In Linux, all entities are described in files so learning how to examine and manipulate them is a good place to start. End users are most familiar with files containing data that they work with on a daily basis. Files can also include such things as end-user programs in addition to operating system programs, program control parameters, hardware device descriptions, and system status information.

Files are stored in directories, which are referred to as folders in a GUI environment. Directories are arranged in a hierarchical tree structure. Everyday workings within a Linux environment will require that the user understand where their files are stored, how to navigate through the directory tree, and how to manipulate files within the directory structure.

This chapter will introduce the commands needed to manipulate files and directories from the Linux command line.

Directory Structure

As mentioned, Linux stores files in directories (folders) which are arranged in a hierarchical or tree structure. The highest level directory is called root and is identified by a slash character (/). All other directories in Linux stem from the root directory. It is admittedly easier to envision the overall structure of the server's directories using a GUI interface such as Gnome. Figure 4.1 is an example GUI display of the directory structure of a Linux server. The figure indicates that the user is in the **/boot** directory which contains two subdirectories called **/grub** and **/lost+found** displayed as folders and numerous files displayed as icons depending upon file type.

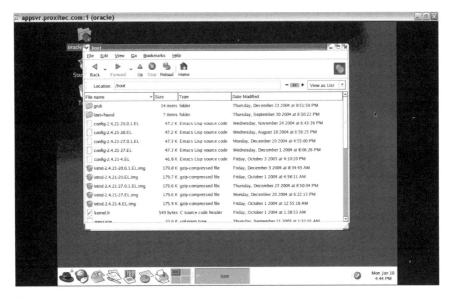

Figure 4.1: *GUI display of Linux directory structure*

Again, this book is written with the assumption that a GUI environment is not available, and that the user is limited to command line, but if you do have a GUI available it may help you understand the directory structure.

The **tree** command can be used to display the directory tree from the command line, but the displayed output can be rather cumbersome to decipher. By default, the **tree** command starts in the current working directory and creates a graphic display of all child directories and the files in each directory.

```
tree
.
|-- System.map -> System.map-2.4.9-e.25
|-- System.map-2.4.9-e.25
|-- System.map-2.4.9-e.3
|-- boot.b
|-- chain.b
|-- grub
|    |-- device.map
|    |-- e2fs_stage1_5
|    |-- fat_stage1_5
|    |-- ffs_stage1_5
|    |-- grub.conf
```

```
|      |-- menu.lst -> ./grub.conf
|      |-- minix_stage1_5
|      |-- reiserfs_stage1_5
|      |-- splash.xpm.gz
|      |-- stage1
|      |-- stage2
|      `-- vstafs_stage1_5
|-- initrd-2.4.9-e.25.img
|-- initrd-2.4.9-e.3.img
|-- kernel.h -> kernel.h-2.4.9
|-- kernel.h-2.4.9
|-- lost+found [error opening dir]
|-- message
|-- module-info -> module-info-2.4.9-e.25
|-- module-info-2.4.9-e.25
|-- module-info-2.4.9-e.3
|-- os2_d.b
|-- vmlinux-2.4.9-e.25
|-- vmlinux-2.4.9-e.3
|-- vmlinuz -> vmlinuz-2.4.9-e.25
|-- vmlinuz-2.4.9-e.25
`-- vmlinuz-2.4.9-e.3

2 directories, 31 files
```

To limit the display to just directories without the files contained in
each directory, the **–d** option can be used. The following is an
example of the output from the **tree** command with and without the **–
d** option.

```
$ tree -d
.
|-- grub
`-- lost+found [error opening dir]

2 directories
```

Though **tree** will give us a quick overview of everything in a directory
we are often only concerned with certain directories or files. Later in
this chapter we'll talk about how to examine a more specific subset of a
directory.

Directory Commands

Here we'll talk a bit about navigating around the Linux file structure.

What Directory am I In?

When navigating around in Linux it is very easy to forget what directory you're in. Don't worry, there's a command to help you find out.

The directory that the user is currently in is referred to as the working directory and can be displayed using the **pwd** (print working directory) command. The **pwd** command displays the absolute path name for the current working directory as demonstrated here:

```
$ pwd
/home/tclark
```

The directory **/home/tclark** is an *absolute path* because it begins with a slash. Absolute paths will refer to the exact same location no matter who types them or where they type them from because the slash specifies that this path is described from the root directory. The opposite of an absolute path is a *relative path* which would refer to a subdirectory of the working directory. Relative paths cannot begin with slashes.

In order to eliminate the need to frequently issue the **pwd** command to determine the current working directory, many Linux users choose to display the working directory within the Linux command prompt. Some Linux administrators even provide this service for their users when they create their Linux accounts. If a user's command prompt does not contain the working directory, the command prompt can be modified by changing the prompt string 1 (**PS1**) shell variable as demonstrated here:

```
$ PS1="[\u@\h \w]\\$ "
[tclark@appsvr /home/tclark]$
```

This example of setting the **PS1** variable also adds the username (**\u**) and hostname (**\h**) to the prompt. This can be very useful if you frequently connect to different hosts and as different users.

In order to avoid having to modify the prompt at each login, the following line of code can be placed within the appropriate configuration file, such as **.bash_profile** for the bash shell, within the home directory. To do this you can use a text editor like **vi** to add the following line to your **.bash_profile** file:

```
$ export PS1="[\u@\h \w]\\$ "
```

Note: Files that begin with a period will not appear when you list the contents of a directory. To see these hidden files use the command **ls −a**

There are even more options which you can put into your **PS1** prompt. While it's nice to keep your prompt fairly short you may find some of the other options useful. Table 4.1 contains a list of values that can be displayed within the **PS1** and/or **PS2** prompt strings:

Symbol	Displayed Value
\!	History number of current command
\#	Command number of current command
\d	Current date
\h	Host name
\n	Newline
\s	Shell name
\t	Current time
\u	User name
\W	Current working directory
\w	Current working directory (full path)

Table 4.1: *PS1 prompt string values*

Creating New Directories

The **mkdir** (make directory) command is used to create a new directory. The directory to be created can be referenced via an absolute path or via a relative path starting with the current working directory.

- Make a directory using an absolute path:

```
$ ls
```

```
examples
$ mkdir /home/tclark/new_dir1
$ ls
examples   new_dir1
```

- Make a directory using a relative path:

```
$ mkdir new_dir2
$ ls
examples   new_dir1   new_dir2
```

The **–p** (parent) option allows creation of a complete directory branch when parent directories do not yet exist. This will actually create both the parent directory and subdirectory specified. In our example that means the **new_dir3** and **sub_dir3** are both created with a single command.

- Make a new directory with a subdirectory using the **–p** option:

```
$ mkdir -p new_dir3/sub_dir3
$ ls
examples   new_dir1   new_dir2   new_dir3
$ ls new_dir3
sub_dir3
```

Deleting Directories

The **rmdir** (remove directory) command is used to delete an empty directory. The directory to be deleted can be referenced via an absolute path or via a relative path starting with the current working directory. The following are some examples of each method:

```
$ rmdir /home/tclark/new_dir1
$ ls
examples   new_dir2   new_dir3
$ rmdir new_dir2
$ ls
examples   new_dir3
```

A directory cannot be removed with the **rmdir** command unless it is completely empty. To remove a directory and its contents you can use the **rm –r** command which will be covered later in this chapter. Be careful with this as you can easily delete more than you had intended!

Renaming directories

Directories can be renamed with the **mv** command. Here's an example of renaming a directory:

```
$ mv new_dir3 another_dir
$ ls
examples   another_dir
```

The **mv** command can also be used to move a directory to another location. This will be covered more later in this chapter when we talk about moving and renaming files.

Navigating the Directory Tree

The **cd** (change directory) command is used to change from one directory to another. As with creating and deleting directories, it is possible to change to another directory by using either an absolute path or by using a relative path referenced from the current working directory.

There are also some special shortcuts that can be used with the **cd** command. For instance, .. refers to the parent directory of the current working directory, ~ refers to the home directory of the current user and - refers to the last directory from which the user changed. The following are some examples of directory navigation.

To demonstrate this without having to type **pwd** after each **cd** we have added the working directory to the prompt on a separate line.

```
$ PS1="Directory:\w\n\\$ "
Directory:/usr/bin
$ cd /usr/bin
Directory:/usr/bin
$ cd
Directory:~
$ cd /
Directory:/
$ cd ~
Directory:~
$ cd examples
Directory:~/examples
$ cd /tmp
Directory:/tmp
$ cd -
/home/tclark/examples
Directory:~/examples
$ cd /home/tclark
Directory:~
```

You might have noticed that the second **cd** command had no directory listed. This will take you back to your home directory from anywhere. This is the exact same result as the **cd ~** command. It is also worth mentioning that when we used the **cd −** combination to take us to the previous directory it printed the current directory before returning us to the previous one.

Listing Directory Contents

The **ls** command is used to list the contents, subdirectories and files, within a directory. There are several options to the **ls** command that determine both the content and order of the listing displayed. Without specifying any options, **ls** displays subdirectory and file names.

```
$ cd ~/examples
$ ls
declaration.txt  gettysburg.txt  preamble.txt
```

Table 4.2 contains descriptions of some of the options that are commonly used to display additional information:

Option	Purpose
-a	Display all files including those which begin with a period (.) which would otherwise not be shown
-l	Display long information include permissions, ownership, size, modification date/time, and file name in the display
-d	Display information about a directory rather than the contents of that directory
-t	Sort the display by date/time

Table 4.2: *ls Command Options*

The following are some examples of the **ls** command using the above options:

```
$ cd ~/examples
$ ls
declaration.txt  gettysburg.txt  preamble.txt
$ ls -al
total 20
drwxrwxr-x   2 tclark    tclark      4096 Jan 13 17:48 .
drwx------   4 tclark    tclark      4096 Jan 13 18:29 ..
-rw-rw-r--   1 tclark    tclark      2230 Jan 13 17:47 declaration.txt
-rw-rw-r--   1 tclark    tclark      1310 Jan 13 17:48 gettysburg.txt
-rw-rw-r--   1 tclark    tclark       360 Jan 13 17:48 preamble.txt
$ ls -alt
total 20
drwx------   4 tclark    tclark      4096 Jan 13 18:29 ..
drwxrwxr-x   2 tclark    tclark      4096 Jan 13 17:48 .
-rw-rw-r--   1 tclark    tclark       360 Jan 13 17:48 preamble.txt
-rw-rw-r--   1 tclark    tclark      1310 Jan 13 17:48 gettysburg.txt
-rw-rw-r--   1 tclark    tclark      2230 Jan 13 17:47 declaration.txt
```

Now that we're comfortable managing and navigating around directories let's take a look at some file commands.

Disk Usage of a Specific Directory

As we create and remove files and directories it is often important to keep track of disk usage. For that we use the **du** (**disk usage**) command.

```
$ du -hs .
2.3M    .
```

Here **du** is called with the options **h** to show the output in a human readable format and **s** to show only the summary of all disk usage in this directory. While we specified the working directory (.) in this example any directory could be given here.

File Commands

Creating an Empty File

Sometimes, it is useful to create an empty file as a placeholder for future content. The **touch** command can be used without any options to create an empty file as follows:

```
$ touch /home/tclark/touch1.fil
$ touch touch2.fil
$ ls -l
total 4
drwxrwxr-x    2 tclark    tclark       4096 Jan 13 17:48 examples
-rw-rw-r--    1 tclark    tclark          0 Jan 13 19:13 touch1.fil
-rw-rw-r--    1 tclark    tclark          0 Jan 13 19:14 touch2.fil
```

The **touch** command also has an option that allows the file timestamp information of an existing file to be changed using the **−t** option. In the following example, the timestamp on the **touch1.fil** above will be changed to January 10 12:00. The date format for this option is given as a string of numbers with two digits each for month, date, hour (in 24 hour format) and minute, so the string for January 10 12:00 would be 01101200. For instance, the user may want to change a group of files in a directory to indicate a particular release date.

```
$ touch -t 01101200 touch1.fil
$ ls -l
total 4
drwxrwxr-x    2 tclark    tclark       4096 Jan 13 17:48 examples
-rw-rw-r--    1 tclark    tclark          0 Jan 10 12:00 touch1.fil
-rw-rw-r--    1 tclark    tclark          0 Jan 13 19:14 touch2.fil
```

A Brief Discussion about Wildcards

Many of the common file and directory manipulation commands, including most of the ones mentioned in the balance of this chapter, will let you use a partial file or path name and substitute a wildcard character for the rest of one or several files. These wildcards can save you a lot of typing, but can also leave you with ambiguous results, possibly even causing the accidental deletion of files!

The two most common wildcard characters are the asterisk (*****) and the question mark (**?**). The *****, commonly called the star, will match any number of any characters within a filename, even if there are none. The **?** will match any single character within a filename.

Here are a couple examples which should make wildcards a bit more clear:

```
$ ls
examples  touch1.fil  touch2.fil
$ ls tou*
touch1.fil  touch2.fil
$ ls touch?.fil
touch1.fil  touch2.fil
$ ls *ch?.fil
touch1.fil  touch2.fil
```

In the last example we see that multiple wildcards can be used within the same statement and both will be applied to the results. The most important thing to remember about wildcards is that they will not just match one but will instead match all files which have the pattern you have described.

Deleting Files

The remove (**rm**) command can be used to delete a file; referencing the file either via an absolute path or via a relative path. Wildcard symbols such as ***** and **?**, can be used to delete files with similar names.

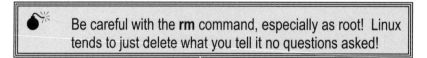
Be careful with the **rm** command, especially as root! Linux tends to just delete what you tell it no questions asked!

Here are some examples of the **rm** command:

```
$ rm /home/tclark/touch1.fil
$ ls
examples  touch2.fil
$ rm touch2.fil
$ ls
examples
```

```
$ touch touch1.fil touch2.fil touch3.fil
$ ls
examples  touch1.fil  touch2.fil  touch3.fil
$ rm touch?.fil
$ ls
examples
```

The **rm** command can be used with the **-r** (recursive) option to remove a directory and its contents. The **rm -r** command, as with other commands which affect multiple files, should be used with caution.

```
$ mkdir -p new_dir3/sub_dir3
$ ls
examples  new_dir3
$ rmdir new_dir3
rmdir: `new_dir3': Directory not empty

$ rm -r new_dir3
$ ls
examples
```

Preventing Accidental File Deletion

A little trick that some Linux users like to implement to prevent accidental file deletion is via the use of an alias. Aliases are similar to variables and can either be set in a session or by placing the command alias in the .**bash_profile** file with a text editor.

By adding this alias the user will be prompted to confirm each file before it is deleted; otherwise Linux, unlike Microsoft Windows, will delete whatever files match the filename criteria without warning!

```
$ alias rm='rm -i'
$ touch touch1.fil touch2.fil touch3.fil
$ rm touch*
rm: remove regular empty file `touch1.fil'? y
rm: remove regular empty file `touch2.fil'? y
rm: remove regular empty file `touch3.fil'? y
```

Deleting Files Using File Properties

When doing some file cleanup operations and it becomes desirable to delete all files within a directory that have not been used or accessed in more than 30 days, the following command example will be useful:

```
$ find . -maxdepth 1 -atime +30 -exec rm {} \;
```

This **find** command locates files which have not been accessed in 30 days, and then executes an **rm** command for each file found. The **find** command can be very useful for performing operations on multiple files. We will discuss **find** in much more detail in chapter 4.

Moving and Renaming Files

The **mv** (move) command will allow you to move or rename files and directories. Linux does not discern between these two functions as renaming can be just considered moving a file to a different name.

The rules for **mv** are similar to those for **rm** described earlier, in that file references can be via a fully qualified path or via a relative path. The use of the wildcard symbols in the filename is also allowed. The following are some examples:

- Move file **example1.fil** from the current working directory to the **/tmp** directory:

```
$ mv example1.fil /tmp
```

- Move file **example1.fil** using the fully qualified path to the **/tmp** directory:

```
$ mv /home/tclark/example2.fil /tmp
```

- Rename **temp1.fil** in the **/tmp** directory to **temp1.xxx** from the home directory:

```
$ cd /tmp
$ touch temp1.fil temp2.fil
$ ls -l temp*
-rw-rw-r--   1 tclark    tclark         0 Jan 13 21:15 temp1.fil
-rw-rw-r--   1 tclark    tclark         0 Jan 13 21:15 temp2.fil
```

```
$ cd -
/home/tclark
$ mv /tmp/temp1.fil /tmp/temp1.xxx
$ cd -
/tmp
$ ls temp*
temp1.xxx  temp2.fil
```

This example demonstrates how by using absolute paths we can perform a command on a directory which is not our working directory.

- Rename **example2.fil** in the current working directory to **example2.xxx**:

```
$ ls
examples
$ touch example1.fil example2.fil
$ ls
example1.fil  example2.fil  examples
$ mv example2.fil example2.xxx
$ ls
example1.fil  example2.xxx  examples
```

So far we've discussed several ways to manipulate files and directories. Since these commands are so powerful you may find that you want to make a backup before you make certain changes. We'll look at how to do this in the next section.

Archiving directories and files

There are several reasons you may want to create an archive of a file or directory. Here are some of the most common ones:

- Archive and compress unused directories to conserve disk space
- Create an archive of a directory and files before an upgrade allowing you to restore the original contents if there is a problem
- Archive a directory before making any major changes
- Create an archive to move several files and folders to another system as one
- Create an archive as a means of software distribution

One of the most useful utilities for archiving a set of files and directories is **tar**. The name **tar** is short for Tape ARchiver because **tar** was originally written to write data to a tape backup device.

The following is a basic example of archiving a directory into a **tar** archive file and also extracting the archive into its original structure.

```
$ tar -cvf examples.tar examples
examples/
examples/declaration.txt
examples/gettysburg.txt
examples/preamble.txt
$ rm -r examples
$ ls
examples.tar
$ tar -xvf examples.tar
examples/
examples/declaration.txt
examples/gettysburg.txt
examples/preamble.txt
$ ls
examples   examples.tar
```

In this example we have demonstrated the two most common uses of **tar**. The first **tar** command combines the **−c** (create) option to create a new archive, the **−v** (verbose) option to list the files and directories it's archiving and the **−f** option to write to a file rather than to tape. Remember that **tar** was originally written for use with tape drives and it still defaults to tape if you do not use the **−f** option.

The two arguments for this **tar** command are the destination file (**examples.tar** in our example here) and the files which should be added to that file. This can be confusing since most other Linux commands take a source argument before the destination. **tar** takes them in the order of destination then source so you can list multiple source files to be archived into a single file. Also not that we have to specify the file extension (.**tar**) if we want our new archive to have an extension. You can name a **tar** archive (typically called a *tarfile* or *tarball*) anything you want, but the .**tar** extension is a widely accepted convention.

In the second **tar** command the **−v** and **−f** options have the same result and the **−x** (extract) option tells **tar** that we want to extract the contents of a tar file rather than create one. We then give **tar** the name of the archive to be extracted and it goes to work restoring our files.

A Warning about Relative and Absolute Paths in tar

As with other commands **tar** can be used with either relative or absolute paths. When specifying the tarfile to be created or extracted there is little difference between these two methods; however, if you use an absolute path when listing files to be archived you might get a surprise when you extract them!

If an absolute path is used to tell **tar** which files to archive, like with the command below the archive will record the absolute path and restore those files to that path, no matter where **tar** is run from or where the tarfile is.

```
$ tar -cf examples.tar /home/tclark/examples
```

If an absolute path is not specified on archiving the files will be extracted into the working directory or the appropriate subfolder of the working directory.

Combining Files

On occasion, the need to combine or concatenate two or more files may arise. The **cat** (short for concatenate) command is a nice simple way to get this done. The **cat** command can take several file names as arguments and will output them all as one file in the order they are listed.

By default **cat** will output the concatenation of the files to the screen but it is easy to redirect the output to a file with the > redirection operator.

In this example we use **cat** to concatenate **file1.dat**, **file2.dat** and **file3.dat** into the file **combined.dat**.

```
$ cat file1.dat file2.dat file3.dat > combined.dat
```

In the next section we'll see how the **cat** command can be useful for more than just putting files together.

Displaying file contents

Oddly enough, the **cat** command is also used to display the contents of a file or to redirect the contents of a file to another command for additional processing, which is presented in further detail in the chapter on shell scripting.

The following is a demonstration of how we can use the **cat** command to display the contents of **preamble.txt**.

```
$ cat preamble.txt
U.S. Constitution: Preamble

We the People of the United States, in Order to form a more perfect
Union,
establish Justice, insure domestic Tranquillity, provide for the
common defence,
promote the general Welfare, and secure the Blessings of Liberty to
ourselves
and our Posterity, do ordain and establish this Constitution for the
United
States of America.
```

The **more** command or the **less** command can be used to display larger files which will not all fit on the screen at once. The **more** command is antiquated and has been largely abandoned in favor of the **less** command. The **less** command actually has more options than **more**. In other words, **less** honors all of the **more** options plus additional options only available with **less**, such as the ability to navigate to a particular line of a file or to a particular percentage of a file. To exit the **less** display, the **q** subcommand can be used.

So since **less** is better than **more** we'll use that. The following is an example of using **less** to display a file called **preamble.txt**. The output has been truncated to save trees and the ellipsis (...) is not part of the **less** output.

```
$ less declaration.txt
The Declaration of Independence of the Thirteen Colonies
In CONGRESS, July 4, 1776

The unanimous Declaration of the thirteen united States of America,

When in the Course of human events, it becomes necessary for one
people to dissolve the political
bands which have connected them with another, and to assume among
the powers of the earth, the
separate and equal station to which the Laws of Nature and of
Nature's God entitle them, a decent
respect to the opinions of mankind requires that they should declare
the causes which impel them
to the separation.

We hold these truths to be self-evident, that all men are created
equal, that they are endowed by
...
Great Britain [George III] is a history of repeated injuries and
usurpations, all having in
direct object the establishment of an absolute Tyranny over these
States. To prove this, let
Facts be submitted to a candid world.

declaration.txt (END)
```

In **less** you can typically use the **arrow keys** to move up and down one line at a time or use the **b** and **space bar** to move up and down (respectively) one page at a time. Remember, when you're done viewing a file with **less** all you need to do is type **q** to quit.

Displaying Beginning Lines of a File

Sometimes a user might have a large file for which they only need to display the first few lines. For instance, perhaps the user would like to see the error code on a dump file and the code and error messages appear within the first fifteen lines of the dump file. The following example demonstrates how to display the first fifteen lines of a file using the **head** command. The **head** command takes a number as an option and uses it as the number of lines to be displayed. The default is 10.

```
$ head -15 declaration.txt
The Declaration of Independence of the Thirteen Colonies
In CONGRESS, July 4, 1776

The unanimous Declaration of the thirteen united States of America,
```

```
When in the Course of human events, it becomes necessary for one
people to dissolve the political
bands which have connected them with another, and to assume among
the powers of the earth, the
separate and equal station to which the Laws of Nature and of
Nature's God entitle them, a decent
respect to the opinions of mankind requires that they should declare
the causes which impel them
to the separation.

We hold these truths to be self-evident, that all men are created
equal, that they are endowed by
their Creator with certain unalienable Rights, that among these are
Life, Liberty and the pursuit
of Happiness. --That to secure these rights, Governments are
instituted among Men, deriving their
just powers from the consent of the governed, --That whenever any
Form of Government becomes
```

In this example and often in use it may seem like **head** is displaying more lines than you asked for. That typically is because the lines are too long for the display so a single line may be continued on the next line.

Displaying Ending Lines of a File

The need might arise to see only the last lines of a file. A good example of this might be an error log file where the user would like to see the last few messages written to the log. The **tail** command can be used to display the last lines of a file, while passing the number of lines to be displayed. The following example requests the last eight lines in the file called **declaration.txt**.

```
$ tail -8 declaration.txt
they are accustomed. But when a long train of abuses and
usurpations, pursuing invariably the
same Object evinces a design to reduce them under absolute
Despotism, it is their right, it is
their duty, to throw off such Government, and to provide new Guards
for their future security.
—Such has been the patient sufferance of these Colonies; and such is
now the necessity which
constrains them to alter their former Systems of Government. The
history of the present King of
Great Britain [George III] is a history of repeated injuries and
usurpations, all having in
```

```
direct object the establishment of an absolute Tyranny over these
States. To prove this, let
Facts be submitted to a candid world.
```

Again it appears we are getting more than eight lines, but this is just the result of long lines wrapping onto two lines.

Display Active Writes to a File

Sometimes you need to go one step further and watch as lines are being written to a file. Perhaps, for example, an application is compressing and copying files to an alternate location, writing messages to a log file called **message.log** as it processes each file. A curious user might want to observe the progress of the application. In this case, the **tail** command with the **–f** (follow) option can be used to read the messages as they are written to a file. The following example assumes that the current working directory is the same directory where the log file resides.

```
$ tail -f  message.log
```

 A clever Linux user can also use the **less** command to display the beginning lines of a file, the ending lines of a file, or to follow active writes to a file like **tail –f** does. See the **man** entry for the **less** command to see how this is done.

These commands are useful for viewing a file in a human readable format. Occasionally you may need to view a file in hex format as shown in the next section.

Display a Hex Dump of a File

While not common, certain circumstances may require a hex dump of a file. The **od** (octal dump) command with the **hex** (**–x**) option can be used to display the file in hex format.

```
$ od -x preamble.txt
0000000 2e55 2e53 4320 6e6f 7473 7469 7475 6f69
```

```
0000020 3a6e 5020 6572 6d61 6c62 0a65 570a 2065
0000040 6874 2065 6550 706f 656c 6f20 2066 6874
0000060 2065 6e55 7469 6465 5320 6174 6574 2c73
0000100 6920 206e 724f 6564 2072 6f74 6620 726f
0000120 206d 2061 6f6d 6572 7020 7265 6566 7463
0000140 5520 696e 6e6f 0a2c 7365 6174 6c62 7369
0000160 2068 754a 7473 6369 2c65 6920 736e 7275
0000200 2065 6f64 656d 7473 6369 5420 6172 716e
0000220 6975 6c6c 7469 2c79 7020 6f72 6976 6564
0000240 6620 726f 7420 6568 6320 6d6f 6f6d 206e
0000260 6564 6566 636e 2c65 700a 6f72 6f6d 6574
0000300 7420 6568 6720 6e65 7265 6c61 5720 6c65
0000320 6166 6572 202c 6e61 2064 6573 7563 6572
0000340 7420 6568 4220 656c 7373 6e69 7367 6f20
0000360 2066 694c 6562 7472 2079 6f74 6f20 7275
0000400 6573 766c 7365 610a 646e 6f20 7275 5020
0000420 736f 6574 6972 7974 202c 6f64 6f20 6472
0000440 6961 206e 6e61 2064 7365 6174 6c62 7369
0000460 2068 6874 7369 4320 6e6f 7473 6974 7475
0000500 6f69 206e 6f66 2072 6874 2065 6e55 7469
0000520 6465 0a20 7453 7461 7365 6f20 2066 6d41
0000540 7265 6963 2e61 0a20
0000550
```

Well that's about it for viewing files, next we'll look at a couple special file operations which may come in handy.

Creating a Symbolic Link to a File

Sometime it's handy to make a file appear as if it is in two places at once. Perhaps you frequently use a file or folder which is buried away in some distant location or maybe you are working on a project with someone else and you both want to see the same file in your home directory. In these cases symbolic links can make your life easier.

The **ln** (link) command can be used to create a symbolic link of a file or directory into another location. In the example below we are making a symbolic link in the working directory which will allow us to access the file at **/var/app/common/parms/app1.par**.

```
$ ln -s /var/apps/common/parms/app1.par ./
```

The **ln** command creates a symbolic link (sometimes called a soft link) from the source file, **/var/apps/common/parms/appl.par**, to a file with the same name, **appl.par**, in the current working directory.

The destination file name need not be coded because it is the same as the source file.

It's important to keep track of which of these files is the original. Thankfully the **ls –l** command will indicate a file is a symbolic link in two ways.

```
$ ls -l app1.par
lrwxrwxrwx    1 tclark    authors        2229 Jan 13 21:35 app1.par ->
/var/apps/common/parms/app1.par
```

The first indication we get that this is a symbolic link is the first letter of the line describing this file is an *l*. We can also see that **ls** has indicated the location of the original file after the file name.

Symbolic links can be edited just like the original file and the permissions of the original file will determine who can edit the symbolic link. Symbolic links can also be removed with the **rm** command without affecting the original file. If the original file is removed the link will fail to work.

Directories can also be linked with a symbolic link. This can often be useful to make a directory appear as if it is somewhere it is not.

Now we'll talk briefly about moving files and directories between machines with the **scp** command.

Remote file copy

The **scp** (secure copy) command can be used to copy files or even entire directories to a remote host. **scp** is a replacement for the **rcp** (remote copy) command. While **rcp** provides the same functionality it is not encrypted and therefore not secure. The **scp** command uses SSH for data transfer, providing SSH level security.

scp takes arguments in the form of **scp *–options source destination***. The most common option is the **–r** (recursive) option which is necessary if you are using **scp** on multiple files or on directories. The *source* and *destination* arguments can specify not only a path but optionally a username and hostname in the format of *username@hostname:path*. If the username is omitted **scp** assumes the username of the current logged in user. If the hostname is omitted **scp** assumes the path provided is on the current system. Typically either the *source* or the *destination* will describe a remote system; however you could use **scp** to move a file or files from one remote system to another.

The following example copies the file **secret.dat** from user **tclark**'s home directory to a directory named **/backup/tclark** on a server named **backup_server** logging in as user **terry**. As indicated below, the **scp** command will prompt for the password for user **terry** on the **backup_server** when the connection is attempted.

```
$ scp /home/tclark/secret.dat  terry@backup_server:/backup/tclark
terry@backup_server's password: password
secret.dat                          100% 1011    27.6KB/s    00:00
```

Conclusions

We covered a lot of ground in this chapter and you should now feel comfortable navigating and manipulating the directory structure within Linux.

In this chapter we first looked at how to examine the directories and files in a file structure. We talked about how to tell what your current working directory is and how you can include it in your prompt so you'll always know where you are.

We then went on to see how to make, remove and rename directories. We talked about moving between directories with the **cd** command and how to view the contents of a directory.

Delving into file manipulation we looked at how to make empty files and how to update the timestamp on an existing file. After seeing how easy it is to delete a file we showed how to make an alias which will cause the **rm** command to prompt us before deleting files.

We talked about several uses for archiving with the **tar** command and saw how to create and extract tarfiles.

We saw how to view the contents of a file, the beginning of a file, the end of a file and even how to combine files. We even talked about using **tail –f** to view lines as they are being written to a file.

Symbolic links were discussed as a way to make files and directories appear in more than one place as well as how to copy things from one system to another.

In the next chapter, some important Linux directories will be investigated in more detail and we will introduce some Linux files of which users will need to be aware.

Important Files and Directories

Armed with knowledge about how to navigate the Linux directory tree and manipulate files, we'll now look at some of the more important files within Linux. This chapter will also provide information on how to identify some of the standard directories created within the Linux directory architecture and where important files are stored within the structure.

Home Directory

Each Linux user is assigned a home directory where they can keep files and build upon the structure by creating their own directories. The user home directories are identified by the Linux login user name and can usually be found under a parent directory called **/home**. If the users on the server are **sally, bill, joan,** and **fred,** the home directory structure would be like the one demonstrated below.

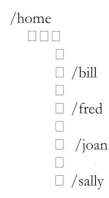

```
/home
   □□□
      □
      □  /bill
      □
      □  /fred
      □
      □  /joan
      □
      □  /sally
```

We mentioned earlier that every Linux system has a **root** user but we do not see a home directory for root here. Since **root** is a special user, **root**'s home directory can be found by itself at **/root**.

Hidden "Dot" Files

There are some files within the home directory that are ordinarily hidden. Hidden files have names that begin with a period; hence, they have been given the nickname of dot files. Hidden files are not displayed by the **ls** command unless the **–a** option is used in the format of **ls –a**.

Table 5.1 below lists some of the more common dot files that users should know about. This is by no means a totally comprehensive list. Additional dot files can be found in the user's home directory; however, some searches may not find some of the files listed here. The files found are dependent upon the applications installed on the server, the utilities that are in use and the command shell that is being used. Since the default shell for Linux is the **bash** shell, the home directory contains the **bash** related scripts indicated below.

File	Description
.bash_history	For users of the bash shell, a file containing up to 500 of the most recent commands available for recall using the up and down arrow keys.
.bash_logout	Script that is run by the bash shell when the user logs out of the system
.bash_profile	Initialization script that is run by the bash shell upon login in order to setup variables and aliases. When bash is started as the default login shell, it looks for the .bash_profile file in the user's home directory; if not found, it looks for .bash_login. If there is no .bash_login file, it then looks for a .profile file.
.bashrc	Initialization script executed whenever the bash shell is started in some way other than a login shell. It is better to

File	Description
	put system-wide functions and aliases in /etc/bashrc, which will be presented later in the book.
.gtkrc	GTK initialization file. GTK+ is a multi-platform toolkit for creating graphical user interfaces, used by a large number of applications. It is the toolkit used by the GNU project's GNOME desktop.
.login	The initialization script that is run whenever a user login occurs.
.logout	The script that is automatically run whenever a user logout occurs.
.profile	Put default system-wide environment variables in /etc/profile.
.viminfo	Initialization file for the Vim text editor that is compatible with vi.
.wm_style	Specifys the default window manager if one is not specified in startx
.Xdefaults & .Xresources	Initialization files for Xterm resources for the user. Application program behavior can be changed by modifying these files.
.xinitrc	The initialization file used when running startx, which can be used to activate applications and run a particular window manager.
.xsession	This file is executed when a user logs in to an X-terminal and is used to automatically load the window manager and applications.

Table 5.1: *Common dot files for the bash shell*

When these files do not exist in the user's home directory, programs that use the files will often use a global default configuration file installed in one of the subdirectories in which the package is installed.

The list below indicates the dot files installed in **tclark**'s home directory.

```
-rw-------   1 tclark    tclark        3773 Jan 13 21:39
.bash_history
-rw-r--r--   1 tclark    tclark          24 Aug 18 11:23 .bash_logout
-rw-r--r--   1 tclark    tclark         191 Aug 18 11:23
.bash_profile
-rw-r--r--   1 tclark    tclark         124 Aug 18 11:23 .bashrc
-rw-r--r--   1 tclark    tclark         237 May 22  2003 .emacs
-rw-r--r--   1 tclark    tclark         120 Aug 24 06:44 .gtkrc
-rw-------   1 tclark    tclark         692 Jan 13 21:35 .viminfo
-rw-r--r--   1 tclark    tclark         220 Nov 27  2002 .zshrc
```

The following is the content of the **.bash_logout** file in **tclark**'s home directory, which is executed whenever logging out of the system. It does nothing more than clear the screen upon logout.

```
# ~/.bash_logout

clear
```

The following is the content of the **.bashrc** file from **tclark**'s home directory. Shell scripts will be presented in a later chapter, but for now suffice it to say that the script looks for a file in the **/etc** directory called **bashrc** and execute it if the file exists.

```
# .bashrc

# User specific aliases and functions

# Source global definitions
if [ -f /etc/bashrc ]; then
        . /etc/bashrc
fi
```

These files primarily affect individual users on the Linux system. Next we'll look at the files which affect the entire system.

Important System Files

Everything in the Linux environment exists in files. It makes sense for users to become familiar with some of the more important Linux system files. Some of these are configuration files, others are devices which Linux makes available through files and some are executable programs.

Table 5.2 below is by no means intended to be an exhaustive list of Linux system files; however, it is a good representation to give some insight into the inner workings of Linux.

File	Description
/boot/vmlinuz	The Linux kernel file. File naming conventions may include release information
/dev/fd0	Device file for the first floppy disk drive on the system
/dev/fd0H1440	Device driver for the first floppy drive in high density mode, commonly invoked when formatting a floppy diskette for that density
/dev/hda	Device file for the first IDE hard drive on the system
/dev/hdc	Commonly, the IDE CDROM drive device file which often is a symbolic link called to /dev/cdrom, the real CDROM driver file.
/dev/null	A dummy device which contains nothing. It is sometimes useful to send output to this device to make it go away forever.
/etc/aliases	Contains aliases used by sendmail and other mail transport agents. Whenever this file is changed, the **newaliases** utility

File	Description
	must be run to notify sendmail of the changes
/etc/bashrc	Contains global defaults and aliases used by the **bash** shell
/etc/crontab	A parent shell script to run commands periodically. It invokes hourly, daily, weekly, and monthly scripts.
/etc/exports	Contains a list of filesystems which may be made available to other systems on the network via NFS.
/etc/fstab	The file system table contains the description of what disk devices are available at what mount points.
/etc/group	Holds information regarding security group definitions.
/etc/grub.conf	The grub boot loader configuration file
/etc/hosts	Contains host names and their corresponding IP addresses used for name resolution whenever a DNS server is unavailable
/etc/hosts.allow	Contains a list of hosts allowed to access services on this computer.
/etc/hosts.deny	Contains a list of hosts forbidden to access services on this computer.
/etc/inittab	Describes how the **INIT** process should set up the system in various runlevels
/etc/issue	Contains the pre-login message, often overwritten by the **/etc/rc.d/rc.local** script in Red Hat and some other rpm-based Linux distributions
/etc/lilo.conf	The lilo boot loader configuration file
/etc/modules.conf	Holds options for configurable system modules

File	Description
/etc/motd	This is the "message of the day" file which is printed upon login. It can be overwritten by **/etc/rc.d/rc.local** Red Hat on startup.
/etc/mtab	Status information for currently mounted devices and partitions
/etc/passwd	Contains information regarding registered system users. Passwords are typically kept in a **shadow** file for better security.
/etc/printcap	Holds printer setup information
/etc/profile	Contains global defaults for the **bash** shell
/etc/resolv.conf	A list of domain name servers (DNS) used by the local machine
/etc/securetty	This file contains a list of terminals where root can login
/etc/termcap	An extensive ASCII text file defining the properties of consoles, terminals, and printers
/proc/cpuinfo	Contains CPU related information
/proc/filesystems	Holds information regarding filesystems that are currently in use
/proc/interrupts	Stores the interrupts that are currently being used
/proc/ioports	A list of the I/O addresses used by devices connected to the server
/proc/meminfo	Contains memory usage information for both physical memory and swap
/proc/modules	Lists currently loaded kernel modules
/proc/mounts	Displays currently mounted file systems
/proc/stat	Contains various statistics about the system, such as the number of page faults since the system was last booted

File	Description
/proc/swaps	Holds swap file utilization information
/proc/version	Contains Linux version information
/var/log/lastlog	Stores information about the last boot process
/var/log/messages	Contains messages produced by the syslog daemon during the boot process
/var/log/wtmp	A binary data file holding login time and duration for each user currently on the system

Table 5.2: *Representative list of Linux files*

Now let's look at the contents of some files from **tclark**'s server. Since these files contain variable information, do not expect the files on every server to look exactly like these.

The following is part of the file **/etc/passwd**. The second field has an **x** as a placeholder for the password. This indicates that the passwords for each user are being kept in a shadow file.

/etc/passwd:

```
# cat /etc/passwd
root:x:0:0:root:/root:/bin/bash
bin:x:1:1:bin:/bin:/sbin/nologin
daemon:x:2:2:daemon:/sbin:/sbin/nologin
adm:x:3:4:adm:/var/adm:/sbin/nologin
lp:x:4:7:lp:/var/spool/lpd:/sbin/nologin
ftp:x:14:50:FTP User:/var/ftp:/sbin/nologin
nobody:x:99:99:Nobody:/:/sbin/nologin
rpm:x:37:37::/var/lib/rpm:/sbin/nologin
sshd:x:74:74:Privilege-separated SSH:/var/empty/sshd:/sbin/nologin
apache:x:48:48:Apache:/var/www:/sbin/nologin
oracle:x:500:501:Oracle Software Owner:/home/oracle:/bin/bash
tclark:x:503:504:Terry Clark:/home/tclark:/bin/bash
```

The fields in this file are separated by colons. In order the fields are username, password (or placeholder), user ID number, primary group ID number, user's full name, user's home directory and user's default shell.

The file system table, **/etc/fstab**, defines parameters for mounting partitions and devices as filesystems. The fields displayed below indicated the device or filesystem to be mounted, the mount point, the type of filesystem, the mount options, dump option, and file check order at boot time.

/etc/fstab:

```
# cat /etc/fstab
/dev/md0                /                       ext3    defaults        1 1
LABEL=/boot             /boot                   ext3    defaults        1 2
LABEL=/bootback         /bootback               ext3    defaults        1 2
none                    /dev/pts                devpts  gid=5,mode=620  0 0
none                    /proc                   proc    defaults        0 0
none                    /dev/shm                tmpfs   defaults        0 0
/dev/hdd1               swap                    swap    defaults        0 0
/dev/hdc1               swap                    swap    defaults        0 0
/dev/hdb3               swap                    swap    defaults        0 0
/dev/cdrom              /mnt/cdrom              udf,iso9660 noauto,owner,kudzu,ro 0 0
/dev/fd0                /mnt/floppy             auto    noauto,owner,kudzu 0 0
```

The **/proc/meminfo** file contains real and virtual memory usage statistics.

/proc/meminfo:

```
# cat /proc/meminfo
        total:      used:      free:  shared: buffers:  cached:
Mem:  2107744256 2088869888 18874368        0 180436992 1587232768
Swap: 1508102144 13074432 1495027712
MemTotal:       2058344 kB
MemFree:          18432 kB
MemShared:            0 kB
Buffers:         176208 kB
Cached:         1544780 kB
SwapCached:        5252 kB
Active:         1391876 kB
ActiveAnon:      790712 kB
ActiveCache:     601164 kB
Inact_dirty:     437124 kB
Inact_laundry:    90216 kB
Inact_clean:      41596 kB
Inact_target:    392160 kB
HighTotal:      1179328 kB
HighFree:          5588 kB
```

```
LowTotal:        879016 kB
LowFree:          12844 kB
SwapTotal:      1472756 kB
SwapFree:       1459988 kB
Committed_AS:   1565668 kB
HugePages_Total:      0
HugePages_Free:       0
Hugepagesize:      4096 kB
```

Next we'll look at some of the significant directories on the Linux system. Some of these will be familiar as the location of the files we've just looked at.

Important Directories

Although organizations have made strides toward consistency via standards such as the **Linux Filesystem Hierarchy Standard (FHS)**, different Linux distributions still have somewhat different directory structures. The following rendering exemplifies a typical Red Hat effort toward standardization of where files are stored according to type and use.

Directory	Description
/bin	All binaries needed for the boot process and to run the system in single-user mode, including essential commands such as **cd**, **ls**, etc.
/boot	Holds files used during the boot process along with the Linux kernel itself
/dev	Contains device files for all hardware devices on the system
/etc	Files used by application subsystems such as mail, the Oracle database, etc.
/etc/init.d	Contains various service startup scripts

Directory	Description
/etc/profile.d	Holds application setup scripts run by /etc/profile upon login
/etc/rc.d	Contains subdirectories which contain run level specific scripts
/etc/rc.d/init.d	run level initialization scripts
/etc/rc.d/rc?.d	Where '?' is a number corresponding to the default run level. Contains symbolic links to scripts which are in /etc/rc.d/init.d. for services to be started and stopped at the indicated run level.
/etc/skel	Holds example dot files used to populate a new user's home directory.
/etc/X11	Contains subdirectories and configuration files for the X Window system
/home	User home directories
/lib	Some shared library directories, files, and links
/mnt	The typical mount point for the user-mountable devices such as floppy drives and CDROM
/proc	Virtual file system that provides system statistics. It doesn't contain real files but provides an interface to runtime system information.
/root	Home directory for the root user
/sbin	Commands used by the super user for system administrative functions
/tmp	A standard repository for temporary files created by

Directory	Description
	applications and users.
/usr	Directory contains subdirectories with source code, programs, libraries, documentation, etc.
/usr/bin	Contains commands available to normal users
/usr/bin/X11	X Window system binaries
/usr/include	Holds **include** files used in C programs
/usr/share	Contains shared directories for **man** files, **info** files, etc.
/usr/lib	Library files searched by the linker when programs are compiled
/usr/local/bin	Common executable application files local to this system
/usr/sbin	Commands used by the super user for system administrative functions
/var	Administrative files such as **log** files, **locks**, **spool** files, and **temporary** files used by various utilities

The contents of these directories will vary from system to system but most of these directories will typically be present. Often when you install software or a new device on a Linux system files will be added or modified in these directories to make everything work.

Conclusions

This chapter has provided an overview of many of the important files and directories on the Linux system. Specific attention was given to the dot files, the hidden configuration files which exist in most user's home directories which control the user's environment.

We then delved into some system configuration files and directories where we can view, and in some cases alter certain things about the system. While the information given here is not enough to fully configure these files it is intended to give an idea of what to find where.

Next we'll look at how the Linux permission structure keeps many of these files safe just like it keeps every user's files safe.

File and Directory Security

Linux file security is quite simplistic in design, yet quite effective in controlling access to files and directories.

Directories and the files which are stored in them are arranged in a hierarchical tree structure. Access can be controlled for both the files and the directories allowing a very flexible level of access.

This chapter will introduce Linux file and directory access permissions and show how those permissions can be manipulated to suit the system requirements.

File Security Model

In Linux, every file and every directory are owned by a single user on that system. Each file and directory also has a security group associated with it that has access rights to the file or directory. If a user is not the directory or file owner nor assigned to the security group for the file, that user is classified as other and may still have certain rights to access the file.

Each of the three file access categories, **owner**, **group**, and **other**, has a set of three access permissions associated with it. The access permissions are **read**, **write**, and **execute**.

A user may belong to more than one group. Regardless of how many groups a user belongs to if permissions are granted on a file or directory to one of the user's groups they will have the granted level of access. You can check what groups a user belongs to with the **groups** command.

```
$ groups tclark
tclark : authors users
```

The **groups** command is called with one argument, the username you want to investigate. As you can see in the output above the output lists the username and all the groups they belong to. In this output *tclark* belongs to the groups *authors* and *users*.

From the information previously presented about file and directory commands, using the **–l** option with the **ls** command will display the file and directory permissions as well as the **owner** and **group** as demonstrated below:

File Permissions, Owner, & Group

The **ls –l** command is the best way to view file and directory ownership and permissions. Now let's look at what each of these permissions do.

File Permissions

File permissions are represented by positions two through ten of the **ls –l** display. The nine character positions consist of three groups of three characters. Each three character group indicates read (**r**), write (**w**), and execute (**x**) permissions.

The three groups indicate permissions for the **owner**, **group**, and **other** users respectively.

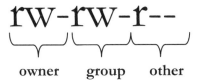

In the example above, both the **owner** and the **group** have read (**r**) and write (**w**) permissions for the file, while **other** users have only read (**r**) permission.

The example below indicates read, write, and execute (**rwx**) permissions for the **owner**, read and execute (**r-x**) permissions for the **group**, and no permissions for **other** users (---).

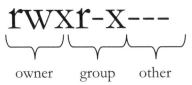

The alphabetic permission indicators are commonly assigned numeric values according to the scheme shown in Table 6.1 below:

Alpha	Numeric	Permission
-	0	No permission granted
x	1	Execute permission granted
w	2	Write permission granted
r	4	Read permission granted

Table 6.1: *Alphabetic permission indicators and their common values*

Then, each three character permission group can be assigned a number from zero to seven calculated by adding together the three individual numeric permissions granted. For example, if the owner has read, write, and execute permissions, the owner's permissions can be represented by the single digit 7 (4+2+1). If the group has read and execute permissions, that can be represented by the single digit 5 (4+0+1). If other users have no permissions, that can be represented by the single digit 0 (0+0+0). These three numbers would then be listed in the order of owner, group, other, in this case 750 as a way to definitively describe the permissions on this file.

Here are some examples of typical file permissions and their appropriate numeric equivalent:

Alpha	Numeric	Permissions
rwxr-xr--	754	**Owner** has read, write, and execute. **Group** has read and execute. **Others** have read only
rw-rw-r--	664	**Owner** has read and write. **Group** has read and write. **Others** have read only.
rwxr-x-r-x	755	**Owner** has read, write, and execute. **Group** has read and execute. **Others** have read and execute.
rw-r-----	640	**Owner** has read and write. **Group** has read only. **Others** have no access.
r--------	400	**Owner** has read only. **Group** has no access. **Others** have no access

Table 6.2: *Alpha and numeric representations of file permissions*

Later in this chapter we will learn how to change file permissions using numbers like these, but first we have to cover a little more background on permissions.

There are some additional abbreviations that can be used with commands that manipulate permissions. These abbreviations are:

- **u: user** owner's permissions

- **g: group**'s permissions

- **o: other**'s permissions

These abbreviations can also be used to change permissions on files. As we will see later, they will allow you to manipulate one level of the permissions (perhaps just the permissions granted to group) without changing the others.

First we'll look a little closer at manipulating the owner and group information of files and directories, then we'll get back to the permissions.

Change File Ownership

As stated earlier in this chapter every file and directory in Linux has an owner and a group associated with it. The need commonly arises where the user or group ownership for files or directories needs to be changed. For example, if user the sally, in group finance is responsible for a number of files and Sally gets transferred to the purchasing group the ownership of the files might need to be changed to marge because Marge is the user who is taking Sally's place in finance. The **chown** command is used to change file or directory ownership.

As another example if a number of files that are currently accessed by the test group are ready for production and need to be changed to the prod group, the **chgrp** command can be used to give access to the prod group.

Actually the **chown** command can be used to change both user and group ownership, while the **chgrp** command can only be used to change group ownership. This command will be covered later in this chapter. When using either **chown** or **chgrp** commands, the system will first check the permissions of the user issuing the commands to make certain they have sufficient permissions to make the change.

Now we'll look at some examples of how to use the **chown** and **chgrp** commands. We'll start with the **chgrp** command, then look at **chown** and then finally see how **chown** can be used to do the work of both!

Change Group Ownership

The **chgrp** command is used to change the group with which a file is associated. The first thing you will need to provide this command is the group which you want to change the file or directory to. After that you can list a single file or directory to be changed or list separate entities separated by spaces. The **chgrp** command will not have any affect on the access granted to the group (the **rw-** in the middle of the three permissions sets) but will change who can use those permissions.

Using the chgrp Command on a File

```
# ls -1
total 12
-rw-rw-r--    1 tclark    authors        2229 Jan 13 21:35
declaration.txt
-rw-rw-r--    1 tclark    authors        1310 Jan 13 17:48
gettysburg.txt
-rw-rw-r--    1 tclark    authors         360 Jan 13 17:48 preamble.txt
# chgrp presidents gettysburg.txt
# ls -1
total 12
-rw-rw-r--    1 tclark    authors        2229 Jan 13 21:35
declaration.txt
-rw-rw-r--    1 tclark    presidents     1310 Jan 13 17:48
gettysburg.txt
-rw-rw-r--    1 tclark    authors         360 Jan 13 17:48 preamble.txt
```

The **chgrp** command works the same for directories as it does for files. In the following example, the group ownership of the directory called **examples** will be changed. Directories are identified by the letter *d* in the first column of the **ls −l** display.

Using the chgrp Command on a Directory

```
# ls -1
total 4
-rw-rw-r--    1 tclark    tclark            0 Jan 13 21:13 example1.fil
```

```
-rw-rw-r--    1 tclark    tclark            0 Jan 13 21:13 example2.xxx
drwxrwxr-x    2 tclark    tclark         4096 Jan 13 21:35 examples
# chgrp authors examples
# ls -l
total 4
-rw-rw-r--    1 tclark    tclark            0 Jan 13 21:13 example1.fil
-rw-rw-r--    1 tclark    tclark            0 Jan 13 21:13 example2.xxx
drwxrwxr-x    2 tclark    authors        4096 Jan 13 21:35 examples
```

You can change the group for multiple files and/or directories by using the **−R** (recursive) option for the **chgrp** command. This is one of the few commands (we'll see two of the others shortly) which use an upper-case R for the recursive option. When applied on a directory the **−R** option will apply the **chgrp** command to the directory and all its subdirectories and files. Care should be taken when using the **−R** option.

Next we'll look at changing the ownership of files.

Change User Ownership

The **chown** (change owner) command can be used to change ownership of a file or directory. The syntax is very similar to **chgrp**.

```
# ls -l
total 12
-rw-rw-r--    1 tclark    authors     2229 Jan 13 21:35 declaration.txt
-rw-rw-r--    1 tclark    authors     1310 Jan 13 17:48 gettysburg.txt
-rw-rw-r--    1 tclark    authors      360 Jan 13 17:48 preamble.txt
# chown abe gettysburg.txt
# ls -l
total 12
-rw-rw-r--    1 tclark    authors     2229 Jan 13 21:35 declaration.txt
-rw-rw-r--    1 abe       authors     1310 Jan 13 17:48 gettysburg.txt
-rw-rw-r--    1 tclark    authors      360 Jan 13 17:48 preamble.txt
```

Just like with **chgrp** we see that **chown** accepts the username of the user who should get ownership and the file or directory to change. Again we could list multiple files or directories here with spaces separating them.

The **chown** command can be used to change the group ownership instead of the user ownership of a file or directory. If you wish to use **chown** to change the group ownership you can list a group preceded with either a colon (:) or a period (.). Here's an example of how to use **chown** to change the group ownership of a file:

```
# ls -l
total 12
-rw-rw-r--   1 tclark    authors      2229 Jan 13 21:35 declaration.txt
-rw-rw-r--   1 abe       authors      1310 Jan 13 17:48 gettysburg.txt
-rw-rw-r--   1 tclark    authors       360 Jan 13 17:48 preamble.txt
# chown :presidents gettys*
# ls -l
total 12
-rw-rw-r--   1 tclark    authors      2229 Jan 13 21:35 declaration.txt
-rw-rw-r--   1 abe       presidents   1310 Jan 13 17:48 gettysburg.txt
-rw-rw-r--   1 tclark    authors       360 Jan 13 17:48 preamble.txt
```

If you wish to simultaneously change both the user and group ownership of a file you can specify the user and group in the format of **user:group**.

In the following example the user will be changed back to *tclark* and the group back to *authors* using a single command.

Using the chown Command to Change File Ownership

```
# ls -l
total 12
-rw-rw-r--   1 tclark    authors      2229 Jan 13 21:35 declaration.txt
-rw-rw-r--   1 abe       presidents   1310 Jan 13 17:48 gettysburg.txt
-rw-rw-r--   1 tclark    authors       360 Jan 13 17:48 preamble.txt
# chown tclark:authors gettys*
# ls -l
total 12
-rw-rw-r--   1 tclark    authors      2229 Jan 13 21:35 declaration.txt
-rw-rw-r--   1 tclark    authors      1310 Jan 13 17:48 gettysburg.txt
-rw-rw-r--   1 tclark    authors       360 Jan 13 17:48 preamble.txt
```

Here we see the user and group has been changed with a single command. Just like with **chgrp** the **chown** command will take the **–R** (recursive) option and apply the **chown** command to a directory and its subdirectories. This should be used with care.

Next we'll look at assigning specific permissions to these users and groups.

Changing File Permissions

Sooner or later it you will need to change access to a file or directory for the user (owner), group or other users. Often permissions are removed to restrict who can update or even view a file. Conversely you may want to grant more permissions to a file to encourage collaboration by allowing more people to view and edit files. It is also not unusual for an application to require specific permissions as a prerequisite for installation.

There are two methods of changing file permissions: with the abbreviations and with the numbers. Both have been described above, so now we'll look at a couple examples of changing permissions using the **chmod** command.

The following example will demonstrate how to change permissions for the **user** (**u**), **group** (**g**), or **other**s (**o**) using the alpha designations (**r**, **w**, **x**) for the permissions preceded by a **+** to add the permission or a **-** to remove the permission. Adding and removing permissions can be combined into a single command as we see below.

Using the *chmod* Command with Alpha Designations to Change File Permissions

```
$ ls -l
total 12
-rw-rw-r--   1 tclark   authors     2229 Jan 13 21:35 declaration.txt
-rw-rw-r--   1 tclark   presidents  1310 Jan 13 17:48 gettysburg.txt
-rw-rw-r--   1 tclark   authors      360 Jan 13 17:48 preamble.txt
$ chmod o+w declaration.txt
$ ls -l
total 12
-rw-rw-rw-   1 tclark   authors     2229 Jan 13 21:35 declaration.txt
-rw-rw-r--   1 tclark   presidents  1310 Jan 13 17:48 gettysburg.txt
-rw-rw-r--   1 tclark   authors      360 Jan 13 17:48 preamble.txt
$ chmod go-w declaration.txt
$ ls -l
total 12
-rw-r--r--   1 tclark   authors     2229 Jan 13 21:35 declaration.txt
-rw-rw-r--   1 tclark   presidents  1310 Jan 13 17:48 gettysburg.txt
-rw-rw-r--   1 tclark   authors      360 Jan 13 17:48 preamble.txt
```

The first example of the **chmod** command here adds **write** permission to the file *declaration.txt* for **other** users. We can see in the second **ls –l** the **w** indication in the second to last column of the permissions in the directory listing. This illustrates the typical format of the **chmod** command where you specify **u**ser (owner), **g**roup and/or **o**ther, **+** to add permissions or **–** to remove them and **r**ead, **w**rite and/or e**x**ecute followed by the filename. Notice that there is not a space on either side of the + or − with the **chmod** command.

In the second example we revoke **write** from both the *group* and *other users*. This demonstrates that we can affect more than one level of permissions with a single **chmod** command. We see this change reflected in the permissions listed in the last **ls** listing.

The next example makes the same permission changes as the previous example, but this time numeric permission designations are used.

Using the chmod Command with Numeric Designations

```
$ ls -l
total 12
-rw-rw-r--    1 tclark   authors       2229 Jan 13 21:35 declaration.txt
-rw-rw-r--    1 tclark   presidents    1310 Jan 13 17:48 gettysburg.txt
-rw-rw-r--    1 tclark   authors        360 Jan 13 17:48 preamble.txt
$ chmod 666 declaration.txt

$ ls -l
total 12
-rw-rw-rw-    1 tclark   authors       2229 Jan 13 21:35 declaration.txt
-rw-rw-r--    1 tclark   presidents    1310 Jan 13 17:48 gettysburg.txt
-rw-rw-r--    1 tclark   authors        360 Jan 13 17:48 preamble.txt
$ chmod 644 declaration.txt
$ ls -l
total 12
-rw-r--r--    1 tclark   authors       2229 Jan 13 21:35 declaration.txt
-rw-rw-r--    1 tclark   presidents    1310 Jan 13 17:48 gettysburg.txt
-rw-rw-r--    1 tclark   authors        360 Jan 13 17:48 preamble.txt
```

Here we see the **666** mode being used to indicate that read (designated as 4) and write (designated as 2) but not execute (designated as 1) are combined (4+2+0=**6**) to grant read and write permissions to user, group and other. We then used the **644** mode to change the permissions so the owner could still read and write, but the group and other could only read.

It can be quicker to modify multiple permissions using the numeric designations but they tend to be much harder to remember. Using the abbreviations you can also easily change the group permissions, for example, without affecting the user or other permissions. The **−R** (recursive) option is also available for the **chmod** command allowing you to modify permissions on a directory and its contents. This should be done with caution as it is easy to lock lots of people out of files and directories, including yourself.

These permissions have a special meaning when applied to directories. We'll take a brief look at that next.

Permissions on Directories

The **read, write** and **execute** permissions apply slightly differently to directories than they do to files. The **read** permission on a directory controls the ability to list the contents of that directory. In this example we'll create a directory and place a blank file in it. We'll then modify the permissions on the directory so the owner cannot see the contents.

```
$ mkdir secret_dir
$ touch secret_dir/my_secret.txt
$ ls secret_dir/
my_secret.txt
$ chmod u-r secret_dir/
$ ls secret_dir/
ls: secret_dir/: Permission denied
$ cd secret_dir/
$ ls
ls: .: Permission denied
$ cd ../
```

We see that we get a Permission denied error when trying to view the contents of the directory when the **read** permission has been revoked. Despite not being able to see what is in the directory we can still change our working directory to that directory.

The **write** permission on a directory behaves somewhat as expected. If a user has **write** on a directory they can create or remove files from that directory **even if they are not the owner of the files**. This is important to note as giving a user, group or other users **write** on a directory with other user's files in it will allow them to delete other users files.

Now we'll give **read** permissions back to the owner and revoke the **execute** permission:

```
$ chmod u+r secret_dir/
$ chmod u-x secret_dir/
```

```
$ ls secret_dir/
my_secret.txt
$ cd secret_dir/
-bash: cd: secret_dir/: Permission denied
```

We can now view the contents of the directory again but look at what happened when we tried to **cd** into it! Not having the **execute** permission on a directory will prevent you from changing into that directory even though you can view the contents. It is understandable how this can cause some confusion.

Setting Default Permissions Using a File Mask

By default, Linux permissions for new directories are typically set to 755 allowing read, write, and execute permissions to **user** and only read and execute to **group** and **other** users. Conversely, file permissions default to 644 allowing read and write access to **user** but only read to **group** and **other**s. These defaults are controlled by the user file-creation mask or **umask**.

A user or administrator may want to change the Linux default permissions by using the **umask** command in a login script. The **umask** command can be used without specifying any arguments to determine what the current default permissions are. The value displayed by **umask** must be subtracted from the defaults of 777 for directories and 666 for files to determine the current defaults. A typical **umask** which will generate the permissions listed in the previous paragraph would be 0022. The first digit pertains to the sticky bit which will be explained further later in this section.

The **−S** option can be used to see the current default permissions displayed in the alpha symbolic format. Default permissions can be changed by specifying the mode argument to **umask** within the user's shell profile (**.bash_profile**) script.

The following are some examples.

Using umask to Set Default Permissions

```
$ umask
0022

$ umask -S
u=rwx,g=rx,o=rx

$ umask 033

$ umask
0033

$ umask -S
u=rwx,g=r,o=r
```

The default **umask** will cause users to create files which any user can read. In many instances where you have a multi-user system this is not desirable and a more appropriate **umask** may be 077. That umask will enforce the default permissions to be read, write and execute for the **owner** and no permissions for the **group** and **other** users.

Special modes

There are a few special permission mode settings that are worthy of noting. Table 6.3 below contains a few of these special settings.

Mode	Description
Sticky bit	Used for shared directories to prevent users from renaming or deleting each others' files. The only users who can rename or delete files in directories with the **sticky bit** set are the file owner, the directory owner, or the super-user (root). The **sticky bit** is represented by the letter **t** in the last position of the **other** permissions display.
SUID	Set user ID, used on executable files to allow the executable to be run as the **file owner** of the executable rather than as the user logged into the system.
	SUID can also be used on a directory to change the ownership of files

created in or moved to that directory to be owned by the directory owner rather than the user who created it.

SGID   Set group ID, used on executable files to allow the file to be run as if logged into the **group** (like SUID but uses file **group** permissions).

SGID can also be used on a directory so that every file created in that directory will have the directory group owner rather than the group owner of the user creating the file.

Table 6.3: *Special permission mode settings and their descriptions*

The following example displays the **SUID** permission mode that is set on the **passwd** command, indicated by the letter **s** in the last position of the user permission display. Users would like to be able to change their own passwords instead of having to ask the System Administrator to do it for them. Since changing a password involves updating the **/etc/passwd** file which is owned by root and protected from modification by any other user, the **passwd** command must be executed as the **root** user.

The **which** command will be used to find the full path name for the **passwd** command, then the attributes of the **passwd** command will be listed, showing the **SUID** permission(s).

The SUID Special Permission Mode

```
$ which passwd
/usr/bin/passwd
$ ls -l /usr/bin/passwd
-r-s--x--x   1 root      root          17700 Jun 25  2004 /usr/bin/passwd
```

Here we see not only that the **SUID** permissions are set up on the **passwd** command but also that the command is owned by the **root** user. These two factors tell us that the **passwd** command will run with the permissions of **root** regardless of who executes it.

These special modes can be very helpful on multi-user systems. To set or unset the sticky bit use the the the **t** option with the **chmod** command. When setting the sticky bit we do not have to specify if it is for user, group or other. In the following example we will make a directory called public which anyone can write to but we'll use the sticky bit to make sure only the file owners can remove their own files.

```
$ mkdir public
$ chmod 777 public
$ chmod +t public
$ ls -l
total 4
drwxrwxrwt   2 tclark   authors     4096 Sep 14 10:45 public
```

We see that the last character of the permissions string has a t indicating the sticky bit has been set. We could also prefix the number **1** to the **chmod** command using the number to achieve the same results. The following **chmod** command will accomplish the same thing as the two **chmod** commands in the last example:

```
$ chmod 1777 public
$ ls -l
total 4
drwxrwxrwt   2 tclark   authors     4096 Sep 14 10:45 public
```

Now let's say we instead want to make a directory which other users can copy files but which we want the files to instantly become owned by our username and group. This is where the **SUID** and **SGID** options come in.

```
$ mkdir drop_box
$ chmod 777 drop_box
$ chmod u+s,g+s drop_box
$ ls -l
total 4
drwsrwsrwx   2 tclark   authors     4096 Sep 14 10:55 drop_box
```

Now anyone can move files to this directory but upon creation in *drop_box* they will become owned by *tclark* and the group *authors*. This example also illustrates how you can change multiple levels of permissions with a single command by separating them with a comma. Just like with the other permissions this could have been simplified into one command using the **SUID** and **SGID** numeric values (**4** and **2** respectively.) Since we are changing both in this case we use **6** as the first value for the **chmod** command.

```
$ chmod 6777 drop_box/
$ ls -l
total 4
drwsrwsrwx    2 oracle    users        4096 Sep 14 10:55 drop_box
```

ACLs – Access Control Lists

Under certain circumstances you may find that controlling permissions on an owner/group level are not sufficient. Perhaps you want to grant just one other user the ability to read a file or maybe you need to share write permissions with several other groups instead of just one.

Some versions and configurations support **ACLs** or Access Control Lists to allow this finer granularity of access control to files and directories. With ACLs you can assign very specific permissions to other users who you don't even share a group with.

Typically a file will not have an ACL. If an ACL has been added to a file you will see a **+** after the permissions string in an **ls –l** listing.

ACLs are very powerful but since they are not typically necessary and support for them is sporadic we will not delve into them in this book. If you want to get more information about ACLs a good place to start would be the **man** pages for **acl,** the **setfacl** command and the **getfacl** command.

Next we'll look at how users can change their active group association.

Logging on to another Group

Every Linux user can be assigned to multiple groups so they can obtain access to whatever files and directories they need to perform their work. Users can determine the groups to which they have access by using the **id** command.

When a user logs on to the system, however, they are assigned to their primary group as specified by the Systems Administrator when the user ID was created. Since Linux only allows a user to be logged into one group at a time, there is a command that allows users to change their current group whenever they need to assume the permissions of another group.

The **newgrp** command allows users to change their current group to any group they have been added to. The **newgrp** command accepts a single parameter consisting of the group name into which the user wished to log.

The following example shows the use of the **id** command to determine the group into which the user is already logged in to as well as all of the groups to which that user has been granted access. In the example, the current **user id** (**uid**) is **tclark** and the current group (**gid**) is also **tclark**. The eligible groups are **tclark** and **authors**.

Determining a User's Current Group and Accessible Groups Using the id Command

```
$ id
uid=503(tclark) gid=504(tclark) groups=504(tclark),506(authors)
```

The next example shows how to switch from the current group of **tclark** to the **authors** group.

Logging into a Different Group Using the newgrp Command

```
$ id
uid=503(tclark) gid=504(tclark) groups=504(tclark),506(authors)
$ newgrp authors
$ id
uid=503(tclark) gid=506(authors) groups=504(tclark),506(authors)
```

Conclusions

In this chapter, information was presented on how Linux file and directory security works through the assignment of **user owner**, **group owner**, and **other user** permissions. The information illustrated how permissions are viewed with the **ls –l** command and manipulated via **chown**, **chgrp**, and **chmod** commands and how default permissions can be assigned via the use of **umask**. Methods for using special permission modes to handle special circumstances were presented.

We touched briefly on Access Control Lists, a useful but rare option for extending the default Linux permissions. We also discussed how to change your current access group to another group which you have permissions to use.

In the next chapter, some of the search capabilities of Linux will be presented to show how they can be used to find files according to specified criteria including some of the access properties we have been discussing here.

Linux Search Tools

Know how to search the server

Finding files using attributes

This chapter will illustrate how to search for files using specific criteria such as size or time last updated. It also includes information on how to search for files containing a specific string or pattern of data. A review of how to search for processes active on the system is also covered.

Using Simple ls Command Options

There will come a time when a user will want to know the last file touched, the last file changed or maybe the largest or smallest file within a directory. This type of search can be performed with the **ls** command. Previously the **ls** command was used to display directories and files within directories, but by using some of the **ls** command options and piping the output of **ls** to the **head** command to limit the number of displayed lines we can find some of these more specific results.

Sample directory

The following home directory is used for the next few examples. Using the **−A** option makes **ls** show files beginning with . but eliminates the . and .. files from the display.

```
$ ls -Al
total 44
-rw-------    1 tclark    tclark      7773 Feb  2 17:11 .bash_history
-rw-r--r--    1 tclark    tclark        24 Aug 18 11:23 .bash_logout
-rw-r--r--    1 tclark    tclark       191 Aug 18 11:23 .bash_profile
-rw-r--r--    1 tclark    tclark       124 Aug 18 11:23 .bashrc
-rw-r--r--    1 tclark    tclark       237 May 22  2003 .emacs
-rw-rw-r--    1 tclark    tclark         0 Feb  3 09:00 example1.fil
-rw-rw-r--    1 tclark    tclark         0 Jan 13 21:13 example2.xxx
drwxrwxr-x    2 tclark    authors     4096 Jan 27 10:17 examples
-rw-r--r--    1 tclark    tclark       120 Aug 24 06:44 .gtkrc
drwxr-xr-x    3 tclark    tclark      4096 Aug 12  2002 .kde
-rw-r--r--    1 tclark    authors        0 Jan 27 00:22 umask_example.fil
-rw-------    1 tclark    tclark       876 Jan 17 17:33 .viminfo
-rw-r--r--    1 tclark    tclark       220 Nov 27  2002 .zshrc
```

Finding the File Last Touched (Modified) in a Directory

The **−t** option is used to sort the output of **ls** by the time the file was modified. Then, the first two lines can be listed by piping the **ls** command to the **head** command.

```
$ ls -Alt|head -2
total 44
```

```
-rw-rw-r--    1 tclark    tclark        0 Feb  3 09:00 example1.fil
```

Using the pipe (|) character in this way tells Linux to take the output of the command preceding the pipe and use it as input for the second command. In this case, the output of **ls –Alt** is taken and passed to the **head -2** command which treats the input just like it would a text file. This type of piping is a common way to combine commands to do complex tasks in Linux.

Finding the File with the Last Attribute Change

The **–c** option changes **ls** to display the last time there was an attribute change of a file such as a permission, ownership or name change.

```
$ ls -Alct|head -2
total 44
-rw-rw-r--    1 tclark    tclark        0 Feb  3 09:07 example1.fil
```

Again we are using the **head** command to only see the first two rows of the output. While the columns for this form of the **ls** command appear identical the date and time in the output now reflect the last attribute change. Any **chmod**, **chown**, **chgrp** or **mv** operation will cause the attribute timestamp to be updated.

Finding the File Last Accessed in a Directory

Beyond file and attribute modifications we can also look at when files were last accessed. Using the **–u** option will give the time the file was last used or accessed.

```
$ ls -Alu|head -2
total 44
-rw-------    1 tclark    tclark     7773 Feb  3 08:56
.bash_history
```

Any of these **ls** commands could be used without the |**head -2** portion to list information on all files in the current directory.

Finding the Largest Files in a Directory

The **−S** option displays files by their size, in descending order. Using this option and the **head** command this time to see the first four lines of output we can see the largest files in our directory.

```
$ ls -AlS|head -4
total 44
-rw-------     1 tclark    tclark      7773 Feb  2 17:11 .bash_history
drwxrwxr-x     2 tclark    authors     4096 Jan 27 10:17 examples
drwxr-xr-x     3 tclark    tclark      4096 Aug 12  2002 .kde
```

Finding the Smallest Files in a Directory

Adding the **−r** option reverses the display, sorting sizes in ascending order.

```
$ ls -AlSr|head -4
total 44
-rw-r--r--     1 tclark    authors        0 Jan 27 00:22 umask_example.fil
-rw-rw-r--     1 tclark    tclark         0 Jan 13 21:13 example2.xxx
-rw-rw-r--     1 tclark    tclark         0 Feb  3 09:00 example1.fil
```

The **−r** option can also be used with the other options discussed in this section, for example to find the file which has not been modified or accessed for the longest time.

Use of the **ls** command options is acceptable when the user is just interested in files in the current working directory, but when we want to search over a broader structure we will use the **find** command.

Using the find Command

*The **find** command can be used to fish for important files.*

The **find** command allows users to do a more comprehensive search spanning the directory tree. **find** also allows the setting of more specific options to filter the search results and when you've found what you're looking for **find** even has the option to do some work on those files.

Finding Files by Age

What if a user wants to determine if there are any really old files on their server? There are dozens of options for the **find** command but the first thing **find** requires is the path in which to look.

In this example we will change our working directory to the **/** (**root**) directory and run the **find** command on the working directory by giving **.** as the path argument. The following command sequence looks for any files that are more than 20 years, 7300 days, old.

Finding Files > 20 Years Old

```
# cd /
# cd /tmp
# ls -ld orbit-root
drwx------    2 root      root          8192 Dec 31  1969 orbit-root
```

By default **find** prints the name and path to any files which match the criteria listed. In this case it has found a file in **./tmp/orbit-root** which has not been modified in more than 7300 days.

You've probably noticed that the date on this file is a bit suspect. While the details are unimportant it is worth understanding that anything on a Linux system with a date of December 31, 1969 or January 1, 1970 has probably lost its date and time attributes somehow. It may have also been created at some time when the system's clock was horribly wrong.

If we wanted to search the **root** directory without changing our working directory we could have specified the directory in the **find** command like this:

```
# find / -mtime +7300
/tmp/orbit-root
```

The command found the same file in this case but has now described it starting with **/** instead of **./** because that is what was used in the **find** command.

The following command sequence will look for some newer files. The process starts in the user's home directory and looks for files less than three days old.

Finding Any Files Modified in the Past 3 Days

```
$ cd ~
$ find . -mtime -3
.
./.bash_history
./examples
```

```
./examples/preamble.txt
./examples/other.txt
./example1.fil
./.viminfo
```

Now we start to really see the power of the **find** command. It has identified files not only in the working directory but in a subdirectory as well! Let's verify the findings with some **ls** commands:

```
$ ls -alt
total 56
drwxrwxr-x    2 tclark    authors    4096 Feb  3 17:45 examples
-rw-------    1 tclark    tclark     8793 Feb  3 14:04
.bash_history
drwx------    4 tclark    tclark     4096 Feb  3 11:17 .
-rw-------    1 tclark    tclark     1066 Feb  3 11:17 .viminfo
-rw-rw-r--    1 tclark    tclark        0 Feb  3 09:00 example1.fil
-rw-r--r--    1 tclark    authors       0 Jan 27 00:22
umask_example.fil
drwxr-xr-x    8 root      root       4096 Jan 25 22:16 ..
-rw-rw-r--    1 tclark    tclark        0 Jan 13 21:13 example2.xxx
-rw-r--r--    1 tclark    tclark      120 Aug 24 06:44 .gtkrc
-rw-r--r--    1 tclark    tclark       24 Aug 18 11:23 .bash_logout
-rw-r--r--    1 tclark    tclark      191 Aug 18 11:23
.bash_profile
-rw-r--r--    1 tclark    tclark      124 Aug 18 11:23 .bashrc
-rw-r--r--    1 tclark    tclark      237 May 22  2003 .emacs
-rw-r--r--    1 tclark    tclark      220 Nov 27  2002 .zshrc
drwxr-xr-x    3 tclark    tclark     4096 Aug 12  2002 .kde
$ cd examples
$ ls -alt
total 20
drwxrwxr-x    2 tclark    authors    4096 Feb  3 17:45 .
-rw-rw-r--    1 tclark    tclark        0 Feb  3 17:45 other.txt
-rw-rw-r--    1 tclark    authors     360 Feb  3 17:44 preamble.txt
drwx------    4 tclark    tclark     4096 Feb  3 11:17 ..
-rw-r--r--    1 tclark    authors    2229 Jan 13 21:35
declaration.txt
-rw-rw-r--    1 tclark    presidents 1310 Jan 13 17:48
gettysburg.txt
```

So we see that **find** has turned up what we were looking for. Now we will refine our search even further.

Finding .txt Files Modified in the Past 3 Days

Sometimes we are only concerned specific files in the directory. For example, say you wrote a text file sometime in the past couple days and now you can't remember what you called it or where you put it. Here's one way you could find that text file without having to go through your entire system:

```
$ find . -name '*.txt' -mtime -3
./preamble.txt
./other.txt
```

Now you've got even fewer files than in the last search and you could easily identify the one you're looking for.

Find files by size

If a user is running short of disk space, they may want to find some large files and compress them to recover space. The following will search from the current directory and find all files larger than 10,000KB. The output has been abbreviated to save trees and ink.

Finding Files Larger than 10,000k

```
# find . -size +10000k
./proc/kcore
./var/lib/rpm/Packages
./var/lib/rpm/Filemd5s
...
./home/stage/REPCA/repCA/wireless/USData.xml
./home/stage/REPCA/repCA/wireless/completebootstrap.xml
./home/stage/REPCA/repCA/wireless/bootstrap.xml
./home/bb/bbc1.9e-btf/BBOUT.OLD
```

Similarly a − could be used in this example to find all files smaller than 10,000KB. Of course there would be quite a few of those on a Linux system.

The **find** command is quite flexible and accepts numerous options. We have only covered a couple of the options here but if you want to check out more of them take a look at **find**'s **man** page.

Most of **find**'s options can be combined to find files which meet several criteria. To do this we can just continue to list criteria like we did when finding .txt files which had been modified in the past three days.

Doing things with what we find

The **−exec** option gives **find** the powerful ability to execute commands on the files found. The syntax is a little tricky but an example is usually all it takes to get it right.

Before using the **-exec** option, especially with a powerful command like **rm** I recommend performing the same **find** without the **−exec**. By doing this you will see exactly which files you will be affecting when you run the final command.

The following is a practical example that finds files less than three days old with the .txt extension and deletes them.

Finding .txt Files < 3 Days Old and Delete Them

```
$ find . -name '*.txt' -mtime -3 -exec rm {} \;
$ ls -lt
total 8
-rw-r--r--   1 tclark    authors        2229 Jan 13 21:35
declaration.txt
-rw-rw-r--   1 tclark    presidents     1310 Jan 13 17:48
gettysburg.txt
```

The **−exec** option allows you to put any command after it. Here we have used **rm** but it is often useful to use this option with **cp** or **chmod**. Within the command to be run there must be two curly brackets {}. **find** will execute the command for each file it finds substituting the file name (and path) where the curly brackets are. Finally the end of the **−exec** option is signaled by an escaped semicolon (\;). The **−exec** option should always be the last option given in a **find** command.

The **find** command is great for finding files and directories but next we'll look at some options for finding other things on the system.

Dealing with "Permission denied" in find

If you use **find** a lot (and you probably will) you will sometimes run into the problem where you get just pages and pages of output like this:

```
$ find / -name '*.txt'
find: /var/lib/dav: Permission denied
find: /var/lib/nfs/statd: Permission denied
find: /var/lib/dhcpv6: Permission denied
find: /var/lib/slocate: Permission denied
find: /var/lib/xdm/authdir: Permission denied
find: /var/lib/php/session: Permission denied
find: /var/log/samba: Permission denied
find: /var/log/ppp: Permission denied
find: /var/log/audit: Permission denied
find: /var/log/squid: Permission denied
...
```

This is **find** telling you there are certain directories you don't have permissions to search. This can make it very difficult to find the useful output of the **find** as it can be mixed in with the permissions errors.

To ignore these (and any other) errors and just get the results of what you *can* find we can use a special redirect at the end of the command. Redirecting output will be covered in more detail in the chapter on shell scripting, but suffice it to say that in this command **2>/dev/null** is redirecting the error output to nowhere.

```
$ find / -name '*.txt' 2>/dev/null
/var/www/icons/small/README.txt
/usr/X11R6/lib/X11/rgb.txt
/usr/X11R6/lib/X11/doc/Xprint_FAQ.txt
/usr/lib/4Suite/tests/Xml/Core/count.txt
...
```

While it would not be a good idea to redirect the error output all the time (usually you want to know when something has gone wrong) in this case of the **find** command it can be very useful.

Finding a String within a Text File

The **grep** command can be used to check a file for a specific string. If **grep** finds that string it will print the line it found it on to the screen. Here's an example:

```
$ cd /etc
$ grep localhost hosts
127.0.0.1        localhost.localdomain    localhost
```

Here we checked the **hosts** file in the **/etc** directory for the word **localhost**. It was found and **grep** printed the line it was found on. **grep** can be very useful for searching through output for errors or anything else which typically has a regular pattern.

Finding the Full Directory Path for a Command

The commands we have been executing exist as files somewhere on the system. The **which** command is used to find the full path of these commands. The following examples will show how you can look for the directory where some commonly used executables are found.

Find the Directory Path for emacs and sort

```
$ which emacs
/usr/bin/emacs
$ which sort
/bin/sort
```

The **which** command takes a single argument of any command. We have shown above the **which** command for **emacs** and **sort**. The result indicates where the binary files for those commands exist on the filesystem.

Finding the Location of Program Binary, Source, Manual Pages for emacs and sort

The **whereis** command can also be used to locate the binary file for commands. Additionally, **whereis** locates the source file and manual page file the command.

```
$ whereis emacs
emacs: /usr/bin/emacs /usr/libexec/emacs /usr/share/emacs
/usr/share/man/man1/emacs.1.gz
$ whereis sort
sort: /bin/sort /usr/share/man/man1/sort.1.gz
/usr/share/man/man3/sort.3pm.gz
```

Finding Strings in Binary Files

If a user encounters a binary file and does not know what it is used for or where it came from, they may gain some insight into its origins and use by searching for character strings within the file. If the **cat** command is used to list a binary file, the user will get a screen full of garbage that will more often than not change the display characteristics. Instead, the **strings** command should be used, as demonstrated in the following examples:

Find All Strings in the Binary File

```
$ strings echo
/lib/ld-linux.so.2
libc.so.6
stdout
getopt_long
__fpending
getenv
...
Copyright (C) 2002 Free Software Foundation, Inc.
This is free software; see the source for copying conditions.  There
is NO
warranty; not even for MERCHANTABILITY or FITNESS FOR A PARTICULAR
PURPOSE.
%s (%s) %s
Written by %s.
%s %s
memory exhausted
```

Again the above output has been abbreviated to save trees, but you can see that there is some useful information here. Just knowing that "This is free software" and that it is copyrighted by the Free Software Foundation can give you some great insight on where this came from and why it might be there.

Finding Occurrences of a String in a Binary File

Here we show how the output of the **strings** command can be piped into the **grep** command to look for specific words within a binary file.

```
$ strings echo|grep GLIBC
GLIBC_2.3
GLIBC_2.1.3
GLIBC_2.1
GLIBC_2.0
GLIBC_2.2
```

This shows how **grep** can be used to limit the output of a command to only lines that contain certain text.

Finding Strings in Multiple Files

Earlier in this chapter we used **find** to search for recently modified files to find a file whose name we didn't know. Now we'll see how **grep** can actually search the contents of files to find specific text.

Finding a File Containing a Particular Text String

```
$ ls -Al
total 12
-rw-r--r--    1 tclark    authors        2229 Jan 13 21:35
declaration.txt
-rw-rw-r--    1 tclark    presidents     1310 Jan 13 17:48
gettysburg.txt
-rw-rw-r--    1 tclark    tclark          360 Feb  3 22:38 preamble.txt
$ grep -ri 'We the people' .
./preamble.txt:We the People of the United States, in Order to form
a more perfect Union,
```

Here we use **grep** with the **–ri** options. The **-r** option causes **grep** to search all files in the specified directory and any subdirectories and the **–i** option tells **grep** to ignore character case. We then specify what string we want to search for. Since this string is more than one word we enclose it in single quotes. Finally we specify where we want to look, in this case the current directory. The **grep** command not only outputs the line which contains the string we asked for, but also prefix it with the file which contains that line.

Find processes

In chapter 8, information will be presented that allows the location of processes by process number, user name, etc. using the **ps** command. Some examples are included here as processes are a typical thing to search for. There will be more discussion of this in chapter 8.

Finding Process Information by Process ID

Sometimes you will need to find more information about a specific process. In that case the **–u** option can be used with the **ps** command to specify the process number

```
$ ps u 4444
USER       PID %CPU %MEM   VSZ   RSS TTY       STAT START    TIME
COMMAND
bb        4444  0.0  0.0  1548   412 ?          S    Jan20   0:00
/home/bb/bb/bin/bbrun -a /home/bb/bb/ext/bb-memory.sh
```

This command will search for process number 444 and return some information about it.

Find Processes Belonging to a Specific User

Using the **–u** option we can look for only processes owned by a specific user. In this example the user's name is **bb**.

```
$ ps -u bb
 PID TTY          TIME CMD
3811 ?        00:00:00 runbb.sh
3814 ?        00:00:00 bbrun
```

```
3815 ?        00:00:00 runbb.sh
3818 ?        00:00:00 runbb.sh
3821 ?        00:00:00 runbb.sh
3822 ?        00:00:00 bbrun
3913 ?        00:00:00 bbrun
4444 ?        00:00:00 bbrun
```

Conclusions

In this chapter we illustrated how to search for files using specific criteria such as size or time criteria using the **ls** command. We then delved into the **find** command and saw how it can be used to look at several different attributes of a file.

We also provided examples on how to search for files containing a specific string or pattern of data. The chapter concluded with a review ways that users can search for particular processes that are active on the system.

In the next chapter we'll learn how to unlock some of the power of the **vi** text editor.

The vi Editor

Advanced servers required advanced editors

Inside vi

The visual editor, more commonly known as **vi**, which is pronounced "vee eye", is a very powerful text editor, created especially for those who are touch typists. While the editor is quite powerful, it can be difficult to learn and cumbersome to use. **vi** was invented long before the introduction of the Windows environment, and it provided powerful features for administrators and programmers using UNIX command line environments.

vi has one outstanding characteristic which makes it a great tool to learn: it's always there. Almost every Linux, UNIX and UNIX-like operating system ships with vi pre-installed. In this chapter, information will be presented on how to use the **vi** text editor to create and modify Linux shell scripts.

*Learning **vi** can be a fight!*

Editor Modes of Operation

For all intents and purposes, the **vi** editor operates in two modes; command mode and insert mode. When **vi** is first invoked, the system will be in command mode. While in insert mode, the user can return to command mode by pressing the escape (**esc**) key. If you're not sure which mode you're in it is always safe to press escape to return to command mode before proceeding.

Commands within **vi** are case sensitive. For example, a lower case **a** performs differently than an upper case **A**.

Starting vi

In order to start **vi** from the Linux command prompt just type the command **vi** followed by the name of the new file to be created or the name of an existing file to be edited. If a new file is to be edited, the user will be presented with a screen with a column of tildes (~) as shown in the following example. This indicates that the user is editing an empty file. The following is an example of an empty file.

```
~
~
~
~
~
~
~
~
~
~
~
~
~
"empty.fil" [New File]
```

Exiting vi

The **:wq** command is used to save the file and exit **vi**. This is actually a concatenation of the write command (**:w**) and the quit command (**:q**). If things are a mess and the user just wants to exit **vi** without saving the file, the **:q!** command can be used. Using just the **:q** command will prompt the user to save the file if changes have been made, so the bang character (!) or exclamation point must be used at the end of the command.

Changing from command to insert Mode

There are several ways to enter insert mode in **vi**, it is just important that we try to remember that when we first enter **vi** we are in command mode (you will forget this frequently, but try.) With the **vi** editor you must enter the insert (**i**) command or the append (**a**) command. The difference in the commands is that **a** inserts text to the right of the cursor, while **i** inserts to the left of the cursor.

Since a new file is presented in the example, either **i** or **a** can be used to get into insert mode. Once in insert mode you can then just start entering text. The following is an example of entering text in the insert mode.

```
We are in insert mode now, so I can type in some text.

See the INSERT mode indication at the bottom of the screen.

~
~
~
~
~
~
~
~
~
~
~
~
~
~
-- INSERT --
```

Once the user has completed entering text, the escape (**esc**) key can be pressed to enter **command** mode again.

There are several ways to enter **insert** mode. For instance, **A** appends text entered to the end of the current line, while **I** inserts at the beginning of the current line. A lower case **o** inserts text on a new line below the current cursor line, while an upper case **O** inserts text on a new line above the current cursor line. Table 9.1 below provides a quick reference to these insert commands and their actions.

Command	Action
a	Append text to the right of the cursor
i	Insert text to the left of the cursor
o	Insert a new line below the current line
A	Append text to the end of the current line
I	Insert text at the beginning of the current line
O	Insert a new line above the current line

Table 9.1: *insert commands and their actions*

Saving the file

Now that some text has been entered, the work should be saved. After pressing the escape key to enter command mode, the write command **:w** is typed in order to write the file to disk. To write the file and quit **vi**, **:wq** would be entered instead. **vi** provides a shortcut to **:wq** where you can instead type **ZZ** to do the exact same thing. Using just the **:w** command leaves the user in **vi** to do further editing. One other option is to write the file to a new filename using **:w! newfilename**. Table 9.2 shows **save** commands and their corresponding actions.

Command	Action
:w	Write the file to disk
:wq	Write the file to disk and quit the editor
<shift>ZZ	Same as :wq
:w! newfile	Write the file to a new disk file called *newfile*

Table 9.2: *Write commands and their actions*

Moving the Cursor Around the File

Many newer versions of **vi**, including the distribution that is used for these examples, allow the user to move the cursor using the arrow keys. Originally, cursor movement was restricted to actions listed in Table 9.3 below.

Command	Action
h	Move cursor one position to the left (left arrow)
j	Move cursor one line down (down arrow)
k	Move cursor one line up (up arrow)
l	Move cursor one position to the right (right arrow)
^	Move to the beginning of the current line
$	Move cursor to the end of the current line
b	Move to beginning of previous word
w	Move to beginning of next word
e	Move to end of next word
G	Move to end of the file
:n	Move to line *n*
Enter	Move to the first word one the next line
ctrl+b	Page backward (up)
ctrl+f	Page forward (down)

Table 9.3: *Cursor commands and actions*

Often it can be quicker to use these commands than the arrow keys, especially since many of them allow the user to prefix the command with a number. For instance, **9b** would move backward nine words in the file.

The vi command syntax can be frustrating at first

Deleting Text

The **vi** editor provides commands for deleting or replacing single characters, single or multiple words, and single or multiple lines of text. Table 9.4 shows some common delete and replace commands with their associated actions. Remember you need to be in command mode to use these.

Command	Action
x	Delete one character of text
r	Replace one character of text with the next character entered
dw	Delete entire word (3dw deletes 3 words)
dd	Delete entire line (3dd deletes 3 lines)
D	Delete from cursor to end of line
s	Switch to insert mode after deleting current character
cw	Delete entire word and switch to insert mode
cc	Delete entire line and switch to insert mode
C	Change (delete and switch to insert mode) from cursor position to end of line

Table 9.4: *Delete or replace text commands*

Searching for Text Strings

The **vi** editor allows the user to search for a text string either forward (down) in the file or backward (up). It also allows a shortcut for repeating the search. A special search capability that comes in handy when writing shell scripts is the ability to search for matching parentheses, brackets, and braces. Table 9.5 below shows some search commands and their associated actions.

Command	Action
/*text*	Search forward in the file for *text*
?*text*	Search backward (up) in the file for *text*
%	With the cursor on a parentheses, bracket, or brace character, you can press the % key to move the cursor to its matching open or close character

Table 9.5: *Search commands and their associated actions*

Cutting, Copying, and Pasting Text

Any of the text deleting commands presented earlier work similarly to the **cut** feature of Windows in that they place the deleted text in a buffer area for potential retrieval at a later time. In Windows, the buffer is referred to as the clipboard.

In **vi** there is a unnamed default buffer and 26 specifically referenced buffers, each identified by one of the letters of the alphabet (a, b, c, d, etc.). In order to reference one of the named buffers, the buffer identifier character is preceded with a single open quotation. So, **"a** refers to buffer **a**, **"b** refers to buffer **b**, and so on.

When one of the delete commands is used, the text is cut from the document and placed in the default buffer. To retrieve text from the default buffer, the upper case **P** command can be used to paste the default buffer before the current cursor line, or the lower case **p** command can be used to paste the contents of the buffer after the current line. Therefore, a **5dd** command followed by a cursor movement and a **P** command would cut five lines of text and place them before the line where the cursor was moved.

Instead of cutting or deleting text, it is also possible to copy text from a file using the **yank** (**yy**) command. The **yank** command presents the option of copying text to one of the specific named buffers. Where **yy** would copy the current line to the unnamed default (unnamed), **"cyy** would copy the current line to the buffer named **c.**

The issuance of multiple **yank** commands to the same buffer without intervening paste commands will result in buffer overwrites. In other words, the user cannot yank line five to buffer **a**, then yank line seven to buffer **a** and expect to be able to paste both lines five and seven somewhere. When a user yanks line five, it is placed in buffer **a** as requested, but when a command to yank line 7 to buffer **a** follows, line 7 will overwrite line five, which is sitting in the buffer. This is one of the reasons for providing multiple named buffers to use for multiple successive yanks. Table 9.6 shows copy and paste commands and their associated actions.

Command	Action
yy	Copy (yank) the current line of text into the default (unnamed) buffer
"byy	Copy (yank) the current line of text into the buffer named *b*
5yy	Copy five lines of text to the default buffer
p	Paste the default buffer after the current cursor line
P	Paste the default buffer before the current cursor line
"bP	Paste the contents of named buffer *b* before the current cursor line

Table 9.6: *Copy and paste commands and their actions*

Undo and Other Useful Commands

Table 9.7 shows some additional miscellaneous commands and their associate actions. Most important may be the **u** command which will undo the last change that was made. In most **vi** editors you can undo several of the most recent commands.

Command	Action
J	Join the current cursor line with the next line in the file
Enter	Split the current line at the cursor position when in insert mode.
u	Undo the last change that was made
U	Undo any changes made to the current cursor line
:r filename	Read the file named filename and insert it below the current cursor line

Table 9.7: *Miscellaneous commands and their associated actions*

vi Reference

For your convenience we have compiled the tables of **vi** commands together for quick reference.

Command	Action
a	Append text to the right of the cursor
i	Insert text to the left of the cursor
o	Insert a new line below the current line
A	Append text to the end of the current line
I	Insert text at the beginning of the current line
O	Insert a new line above the current line

Insert Commands

To return to command mode from insert mode use the **escape** key.

Command	Action
:w	Write the file to disk
:wq	Write the file to disk and quit the editor
<shift>ZZ	Same as :wq
:w! newfile	Write the file to a new disk file called *newfile*

Write Commands:

Command	Action
h	Move cursor one position to the left (left arrow)
j	Move cursor one line down (down arrow)
k	Move cursor one line up (up arrow)
l	Move cursor one position to the right (right arrow)
^	Move to the beginning of the current line
$	Move cursor to the end of the current line
b	Move to beginning of previous word
w	Move to beginning of next word
e	Move to end of next word
G	Move to end of the file
:n	Move to line *n*
Enter	Move to the first word one the next line
ctrl+b	Page backward (up)
ctrl+f	Page forward (down)

Cursor Movement:

Command	Action
x	Delete one character of text
r	Replace one character of text with the next character entered
dw	Delete entire word (3dw deletes 3 words)
dd	Delete entire line (3dd deletes 3 lines)
D	Delete from cursor to end of line
s	Switch to insert mode after deleting current character
cw	Delete entire word and switch to insert mode
cc	Delete entire line and switch to insert mode
C	Change (delete and switch to insert mode) from cursor position to end of line

Delete and Replace Commands

Command	Action
/text	Search forward in the file for *text*
?text	Search backward (up) in the file for *text*
%	With the cursor on a parentheses, bracket, or brace character, you can press the % key to move the cursor to its matching open or close character

Search Commands

Command	Action
yy	Copy (yank) the current line of text into the default buffer
"byy	Copy (yank) the current line of text into the buffer named *b*
5yy	Copy five lines of text to the default buffer
p	Paste the default buffer after the current cursor line
P	Paste the default buffer before the current cursor line
"bP	Paste the contents of named buffer *b* before the current cursor line

Copy and Paste Commands

Command	Action
J	Join the current cursor line with the next line in the file
Enter	Split the current line at the cursor position when in insert mode.
u	Undo the last change that was made
U	Undo any changes made to the current cursor line
:r filename	Read the file named filename and insert it below the current cursor line

Undo and Miscellaneous Commands

Conclusions

In this chapter we saw how to edit files with the **vi** text editor. While the **vi** commands may seem confusing at first once you get used to them they are actually quite powerful!

Entire books have been written on the **vi** editor and we have really just scraped the surface here, but it should be enough for you to get started. It might even get you out of a pinch some day when you don't have a graphical editor available.

We'll get the chance to put our newly found **vi** skills to work for writing shell scripts in the next chapter.

Shell Scripts

Shell script seem like magic at first

Programming with Linux

In this chapter, additional Linux commands will be introduced and used to show how to build programs called shell scripts. Shell scripting is the topic of my next book, *Oracle Shell Scripting: Linux and UNIX Programming for Oracle* in which I cover much of this information in great detail. If you are interested in shell scripting you might want to pick it up! Though some of the examples use Oracle, much of the books content is applicable for anyone interested in the topic. Here we will just cover things briefly in order to give a general idea about how scripts are created to perform functions that are repeated on a periodic basis.

Instead of jumping directly into the creation of scripts, there are a few additional topics that should be presented first as well as some questions that need to be answered.

What is a shell?

As described earlier in this book a shell provides a command interpreter environment for giving instructions to the Linux kernel via English-like commands. There are a number of different shell environments available in Linux. In order to determine which shell environments are available on a user's version of Linux, the following command should be issued:

```
$ cat /etc/shells
/bin/sh
/bin/bash
/sbin/nologin
/bin/bash2
/bin/ash
/bin/bsh
/bin/ksh
/bin/tcsh
/bin/csh
/bin/zsh
```

The resulting list indicates that there are several shells available on this server such as the Bourne shell (**sh**), the Bourne Again shell (**bash**), the Korn shell (**ksh**) and the C-shell (**csh**), among others. In Linux, the **bash** shell is normally the default shell.

To determine the default shell to which the system is currently set, the following command should be run:

```
$ echo $SHELL
/bin/bash
```

As predicted, the **bash** shell is the current default.

The shell is a command language interpreter that executes commands read from the standard input device such as a keyboard or from a plain text file.

A shell can be compared to the Microsoft Windows command prompt, which also executes commands issued from the keyboard or from text (**.bat**) files; however, the shell environment is much more robust and feature-rich than its Windows counterpart.

Command Aliases

Aliases are the shell scripts little cousin. A shell script, as we will see shortly, is a file which contain a list of commands. Aliases, in contrast, can be used to perform complex commands but are set in the shell like environmental variables.

If you find yourself frequently using a fairly complicated command like the one below and want to be able to run it without typing the whole thing you can use the **alias** command to set up a shortcut.

```
$ alias alert='tail -200 /u01/installed/software/mypgm/alert.log|more'
```

Now you can execute this whole command simply by typing **alert**. Many of the features we will discuss when talking about shell scripting are available in aliases including the **pipe** (|) used to send the output of one command to the input of another.

A small set of well written aliases can save you a lot of keystrokes, just be careful not to make aliases with the same name as commands you use unless you want the alias to replace that command when you type it.

Not just any clown can learn Linux shell scripts

Why use shell scripts?

Since the shell is capable of reading commands from a file, called a script, it becomes a simple task to use a basic text editor like **vi** to build scripts to simplify frequently performed tasks and to automate the performance of those tasks.

Programming simple or complex actions into shell scripts can simplify repetitive administrative and maintenance functions within the Linux environment.

Getting Started with a Simple Shell Script

A shell script gets executed just as if you were at the keyboard typing commands. Because of this we will demonstrate many of the capabilities of shell scripts right at the command line. Once tested at the command line, these commands can be moved into shell scripts. Here's an example of a simple shell script:

```
#!/bin/bash
# A simple shell script to output the time
echo "The current date and time is `date`"
```

This three line script starts with two comments (anything following a **#** is ignored by the shell), then has an **echo** command which outputs some text and the current date with the **date** command.

If you enter these lines into a text file called *what_time.sh* you can then execute it as a shell script with the **bash** command:

```
$ bash what_time.sh
The current date and time is Fri Sep 15 14:58:23 EDT 2006
```

The **.sh** extensions is not necessary but is the conventional way to indicate a **bash** shell script.

If we want to make things even easier we can change the execution privileges on this shell script so we don't even need the **bash** command to run it.

```
$ chmod u+x what_time.sh
$ ./what_time.sh
The current date and time is Fri Sep 15 15:18:56 EDT 2006
```

This works because the first line of our *what_time.sh* shell script is special. When the first line of a shell script begins with **#!** it is used as a hint to indicate what command should be used to execute this script. When Linux processes this script for execution it sees this hint and uses **bash** to execute it.

We'll spend the rest of this chapter looking at many of the hundreds of commands you can use in shell scripts, but remember, shell scripts don't have to be complicated! They may just take the place of a couple commands that you run frequently or a long command that you have troubles remembering.

Shell variables

Shells provide an abundance of useful built-in information that can be referenced in globally available variables. In order to see the information provided in a shell, the **set** command can be run as demonstrated below.

Here's a partial output of the **set** command:

```
$ set
BASH=/bin/bash
BASH_VERSINFO=([0]="2" [1]="05b" [2]="0" [3]="1" [4]="release"
[5]="i386-redhat-linux-gnu")
BASH_VERSION='2.05b.0(1)-release'
GROUPS=()
G_BROKEN_FILENAMES=1
HISTFILE=/home/tclark/.bash_history
HISTFILESIZE=1000
HISTSIZE=1000
HOME=/home/tclark
HOSTNAME=appsvr.mytec.com
OSTYPE=linux-gnu
PATH=/usr/kerberos/bin:/usr/local/bin:/bin:/usr/bin:/usr/X11R6/bin:/
home/tclark/bin
...
PS1='[\u@\h \W]\$ '
PS2='> '
PS4='+ '
PWD=/home/tclark
SHELL=/bin/bash
SHLVL=1
SSH_ASKPASS=/usr/libexec/openssh/gnome-ssh-askpass
SSH_CLIENT='206.107.231.178 1379 22'
SSH_CONNECTION='206.107.231.178 1379 192.168.15.105 22'
SSH_TTY=/dev/pts/0
SUPPORTED=en_US.UTF-8:en_US:en
TERM=vt100
UID=503
USER=tclark
_=clear
```

The contents of a shell variable can be displayed by using the **echo** command and prefacing the variable name with a dollar sign as demonstrated below. Shell variables are referenced using all capital letters.

```
$ echo $TERM
```

```
vt100
$ echo $USER
tclark
$ echo $HOSTNAME ... $LOGNAME
appsvr.mytec.com ... tclark
```

There are also some special built-in variables that can be useful when creating shell scripts. Some of them are listed in Table 8.1 below.

Built-in Variable	Description
$#	The total number of arguments passed to a shell script on the command line.
$*	All arguments passed to the shell script.
$0	The command (script) invoked on the command line.
$1 - $9	The first through ninth arguments passed to the shell script from the command line.

Table 8.1: *Shell built-in variables*

These variables are provided by the shell, but when programming shell scripts you may need additional variables. Next we'll look at variables you can make yourself, user defined variables.

User Defined Variables

Shells also allow the creation of variables for use within scripts (local variables) and for passing between scripts (global variables). User variables are traditionally created using lower-case characters though they can be any case you want.

The creation of a variable requires merely choosing a lower-case name for the variable and giving it a value using an equal (=) sign. There should be no spaces on either side of the equal sign. If there are spaces or special characters in the contents of your variable you should enclose the variable in single quotes.

The **unset** command can be used to nullify the value of a previous set variable. The following are some examples:

```
$ myname='Terry Clark'
$ echo myname
```

```
myname
$ echo $myname
Terry Clark
$ unset myname
$ echo $myname

$ number=10
$ echo $number
10
```

In this example we see that in order to *set* the contents of a variable we just give the variable name, but if we want to *retrieve* the contents of a variable we must use a dollar sign (**$**) before the variable name.

The variables created above are local variables available only to the current shell. Variables must be **export**ed if they are to become global so they can be referenced by other shell scripts. The following example shows the creation of global user variables.

```
$ myname=Terry
$ export myname
```

In the **bash** shell we can combine these two lines into one and use the following command to set and **export** a variable:

```
$ export myname=Terry
```

Variables are great for storing information. Later we'll see how we can use variables to make decisions and loops, but first we've got a little more basic ground to cover.

Evaluating Expressions

Shells can evaluate complex expressions and allow the user to perform math functions. The following examples demonstrate some simplistic math using the **expr** command:

```
$ expr 6 + 3
9
$ expr 6 + 3 + 8
17
$ expr 8 - 2
6
$ expr 12 / 3
```

```
4
$ expr 15 \* 3
45
$ expr 20 % 3
2
$ echo `expr 15 + 3`
18
```

The example above shows not only the common use of **expr** but some of the exceptions you may find in the **expr** command, such as:

The multiplication example uses an escape character (\) before the *** so that the *** is not interpreted as a wildcard symbol.

"**20 % 3**" is read as 20 mod 3 and yields the remainder when 20 is divided by 3.

The last example uses backward quote signs (`) to enclose the command. The command within the backward quotes is executed and the result echoed to the screen.

Using Quotes in Shell Scripts

Since the use of the backward quote (Formally, a "grave", pronounced Gra-vee) or **backtick** has been mentioned, this is probably a good time to explain the rules regarding the use of quotes:

- Double quote ("): Variables are expanded when enclosed in double quotes

- Single quote ('): Variables within single quotes are not expanded

- Backward quote (`): Commands within backward quotes are executed and their output substituted into that location.

The following examples should help make the differences between the types of quotes more evident.

```
$ myname='Terry Clark'
$ echo 'My name is $myname'
My name is $myname
$ echo "My name is $myname"
My name is Terry Clark
```

```
$ echo 'The name of this computer is `hostname`'
The name of this computer is `hostname`
$ echo "The name of this computer is `hostname`"
The name of this computer is appsvr.mytec.com
```

So we see that when enclosed in single quotes text is treated very literally, but when enclosed in double quotes variables and commands in backward quotes are evaluated and their values output.

Exit Status

Whenever a command or shell script completes successfully, it sets a hidden status code of zero. If the command is unsuccessful, it sets a nonzero hidden status code. This completion status code is known as the **exit status**. The **exit status** of the last command or script that was run is contained in the special shell variable, **$?**.

Most of the time we never look at this value and instead check to see if the command did what we want or look for errors in the output of commands. In a shell script, however, we may want to check the **exit status** to make sure everything is going OK. The **exit status** of the last command can be displayed as follows:

```
$ ls
example1.fil   example2.xxx   examples   test.bsh   umask_example.fil
$ echo $?
0
$ ls *.txt
ls: *.txt: No such file or directory
$ echo $?
1
```

The conditional statements shown later in this section can be used to make decisions based on the **exit status** of the previous command. This can be useful for handling and reporting errors in a shell script.

The read Statement

The **read** command is used to accept input from standard input such as a keyboard and store it into variables. This is useful if you want to prompt for input from the user running your script.

The **read** command reads one line from the standard input and the first word is assigned to the first variable, the second word to the second variable, and so on, with leftover words assigned to the last variable. If there are fewer words read from the input stream than variables, the remaining variables are assigned empty values.

Here are some examples of the **read** command:

```
$ read name1 name2
Terry Clark
$ echo $name2
Clark
$ echo "Name1: $name1    Name2: $name2"
Name1: Terry    Name2: Clark
$ read fullname
Terry L. Clark
$ echo $fullname
Terry L. Clark
```

The **–p** option can be used to specify a prompt to be displayed to the user. The prompt can be used to request that the user enter specific information. The following is an example of using **read** with the **–p** option to prompt the user for input:

```
$ read -p "Enter your name please: "  fullname
Enter your name please: Terry Clark
$ echo $fullname
Terry Clark
```

Now you can start to see how we can make an interactive shell script which prompts the user for input. Sometimes we want to collect information when the shell script is started rather than once it is running. For that type of information **command line arguments** can be used.

Command Line Arguments

Arguments or parameters can be passed to the script from the command line that invoked the script just like we have been passing arguments to commands. Arguments passed to the script are available in special shell variables which are referenced by number. The first argument can be referenced using the variable *$1*, the second argument using *$2*, etc. The *$0* variable is special and contains the name of the command used to invoke the script or command name. The following is an example of using command line arguments.

```
#
#  This script accepts a user's first and last name and
#  displays the current login username, hostname, and home
#  directory.
#

firstname=$1
lastname=$2

echo " "
echo "  Hello $1"
echo "  You are logged in as: $USER  on server: $HOSTNAME"
echo "  Your home directory is: $HOME "
echo "  Thank you, $firstname $lastname for invoking the $0 command"
echo " "
```

Note that anything after a pound sign (**#**) in a shell script is a comment and will be ignored when the script is run.

If we were to run the above script here is what you would get as a result:

```
$ ./mylogin Terry Clark

  Hello Terry
  You are logged in as: tclark  on server: appsvr.mytec.com
  Your home directory is: /home/tclark
  Thank you, Terry Clark for invoking the ./mylogin command
```

We can see how the script has captured the input and substituted the **$0**, **$1** and **$2** variables into the context of the output. We have also used some of the global shell variables discussed earlier like $USER, $HOSTNAME and $HOME.

Sometimes the input you're looking for won't come from a user at a keyboard but rather from a file or from the output of another command. Other times you may want to output information to an output file or a log. Next we'll look at how to do these things within your shell commands and scripts.

Redirection of Standard Input & Output

In Linux, the standard input device is the keyboard, and the standard output device is the display screen. These are the defaults for input and output; however, Linux does allow the redirection of both standard input and output to files. In other words, Linux accepts input from files and can direct output to files.

Three symbols are used to indicate redirection to Linux. Table 8.2 below shows the meanings of the symbols:

Symbol	Meaning
<	Accept input from a file instead of the keyboard
>	Send output to a file instead of the display device (overwriting the file)
>>	Append output to the end of the indicated file. For example, keep a log file.

Table 8.2: *Redirection symbols and their meanings*

The following is an example of redirecting command output to a file using the **>** symbol. We then examine the file with the **cat** command.

```
$ ls -alt > dir.lst
$ cat dir.lst
total 68
drwx------    4 tclark    tclark      4096 Feb 24 23:27 .
-rw-rw-r--    1 tclark    tclark         0 Feb 24 23:27 dir.lst
-rw-------    1 tclark    tclark     11629 Feb 24 21:24
.bash_history
-rwxrwxr-x    1 tclark    tclark       325 Feb 24 21:17 mylogin
-rw-------    1 tclark    tclark      4151 Feb 24 21:17 .viminfo
-rwxrwxr-x    1 tclark    tclark       208 Feb 19 22:52 test.bsh
drwxrwxr-x    2 tclark    authors     4096 Feb  3 23:11 examples
-rw-rw-r--    1 tclark    tclark         0 Feb  3 09:00 example1.fil
-rw-r--r--    1 tclark    authors        0 Jan 27 00:22
umask_example.fil
drwxr-xr-x    8 root      root        4096 Jan 25 22:16 ..
-rw-rw-r--    1 tclark    tclark         0 Jan 13 21:13 example2.xxx
-rw-r--r--    1 tclark    tclark       120 Aug 24  2004 .gtkrc
-rw-r--r--    1 tclark    tclark        24 Aug 18  2004 .bash_logout
-rw-r--r--    1 tclark    tclark       191 Aug 18  2004
.bash_profile
-rw-r--r--    1 tclark    tclark       124 Aug 18  2004 .bashrc
-rw-r--r--    1 tclark    tclark       237 May 22  2003 .emacs
-rw-r--r--    1 tclark    tclark       220 Nov 27  2002 .zshrc
```

```
drwxr-xr-x    3 tclark    tclark       4096 Aug 12  2002 .kde
```

If instead we want to add on to the end of a file the **>>** symbol can be used. Here we are placing the current time at the end of the *time.txt* file then examining the file with **cat**:

```
$ date >> time.txt
$ date >> time.txt
$ date >> time.txt
$ cat time.txt
Thu Feb 24 23:31:22 MST 2005
Thu Feb 24 23:31:36 MST 2005
Thu Feb 24 23:31:50 MST 2005
```

Here is how a file can be redirected *into* a command. In this case we're using the **dir.lst** file from the example above.

```
$ less < dir.lst
total 68
drwx------    4 tclark    tclark       4096 Feb 24 23:27 .
-rw-rw-r--    1 tclark    tclark          0 Feb 24 23:27 dir.lst
-rw-------    1 tclark    tclark      11629 Feb 24 21:24
.bash_history
-rwxrwxr-x    1 tclark    tclark        325 Feb 24 21:17 mylogin
-rw-------    1 tclark    tclark       4151 Feb 24 21:17 .viminfo
-rwxrwxr-x    1 tclark    tclark        208 Feb 19 22:52 test.bsh
drwxrwxr-x    2 tclark    authors      4096 Feb  3 23:11 examples
-rw-rw-r--    1 tclark    tclark          0 Feb  3 09:00 example1.fil
-rw-r--r--    1 tclark    authors         0 Jan 27 00:22
umask_example.fil
drwxr-xr-x    8 root      root         4096 Jan 25 22:16 ..
-rw-rw-r--    1 tclark    tclark          0 Jan 13 21:13 example2.xxx
-rw-r--r--    1 tclark    tclark        120 Aug 24  2004 .gtkrc
-rw-r--r--    1 tclark    tclark         24 Aug 18  2004 .bash_logout
-rw-r--r--    1 tclark    tclark        191 Aug 18  2004
.bash_profile
-rw-r--r--    1 tclark    tclark        124 Aug 18  2004 .bashrc
-rw-r--r--    1 tclark    tclark        237 May 22  2003 .emacs
-rw-r--r--    1 tclark    tclark        220 Nov 27  2002 .zshrc
drwxr-xr-x    3 tclark    tclark       4096 Aug 12  2002 .kde
(END)
```

Sometimes we want to cut out the middle man, avoid using files, and redirect output directly from one command to another. That's where the **pipe** comes in.

Pipes

The **pipe** can be used to pass the output from one command or program to another command or program without creating an intermediate file. The use of **pipes** is a convenient way to string together multiple commands on a command line. The **pipe** symbol is the vertical bar (|), which is placed between commands to invoke a **pipe**.

To see the files in the current working directory that have *.fil* as the file name extension, a pipe could be formed between the **ls** and **grep** commands as follows:

```
$ ls -l|grep .fil
-rw-rw-r--     1 tclark    tclark         0 Feb  3 09:00 example1.fil
-rw-r--r--     1 tclark    authors        0 Jan 27 00:22
umask_example.fil
```

It's important to note that the **grep** command here is not only looking at the file name but is actually looking for the string *.fil* anywhere in the lines of the **ls –l** output.

The following more complicated **pipe** example show the current processes (**ps –ef**), redirects the list of processes to filter for only ones with **root** in the output (**grep root**), and counts the number of remaining lines with the word count command (**wc –l**). The resulting string of commands returns the total number of current **root** processes.

```
$ ps -ef|grep root|wc -l
    38
```

This shows how **pipes** can be used to combine multiple commands to get some fairly sophisticated results.

Conditional Statements

An important aspect of programming is being able to determine if a condition is true or false and then perform specific actions depending upon the outcome of the condition test. This can be especially useful when used with the **exit status** of the previous command.

Shell scripting supplies several ways of testing conditions and then performing specific actions. Some examples of condition statements are the **if** condition, the **case** statement and the **test** or **expression** statement. Conditions are also tested in the **while** loop and the **until** loop and specific actions are repeated.

The if condition

The simple form of the **if** statement consists of the **if** condition, a **then** statement followed by commands to be executed when the **if** condition is true, and the **fi** statement (**if** spelled backwards) which ends the **if** statement. The condition usually consists of a simple comparison between two values, such as A=B or number=5. The following is a simple **if** conditional statement.

```
$ x=3
$ y=9
$ if [ $x -lt $y ]
>      then
>          echo " "
>          echo "  x=${x} which is less than y=${y}"
>          echo " "
> fi

 x=3 which is less than y=9
```

The simple **if** statement also provides an **else** clause which allows the execution of commands when the condition is false. The following is an example of a simple **if-then-else** statement.

```
$ x=3
$ y=2
$ if [ $x -lt $y ]
```

```
>    then
>        echo "   "
>        echo "  ${x} is less than ${y}"
>        echo "   "
>    else
>        echo "   "
>        echo "  ${x} is not less than ${y}"
>        echo "   "
> fi

  3 is not less than 2
```

It is also possible to create compound conditional statements by using one or more **else if** (**elif**) clauses. If the first condition is false, then subsequent **elif** statements are checked. When an **elif** condition is found to be true, the statements following the associated **then** statement are executed.

If the first condition and subsequent **elif** conditions are false, statements following the **else** statement, if present, are executed. The following script shows an example of compound conditional **if** statements.

```
$ x=5
$ y=5
$ if [ $x -lt $y ]
>    then
>        echo "   "
>        echo "  ${x} is less than ${y}"
>        echo "   "
>    elif [ $x -eq $y ]
>    then
>        echo "   "
>        echo "  ${x} is equal to ${y}"
>        echo "   "
>    else
>        echo "   "
>        echo "  ${x} is greater than ${y}"
>        echo "   "
> fi

  5 is equal to 5
```

Now we'll run the exact same script but with different values for **x** and **y** so we can test for another result.

```
$ x=5
$ y=3
$
$ if [ $x -lt $y ]
>     then
>       echo "   "
>       echo "   ${x} is less than ${y}"
>       echo "   "
>     elif [ $x -eq $y ]
>       then
>         echo "   "
>         echo "   ${x} is equal to ${y}"
>         echo "   "
>     else
>       echo "   "
>       echo "   ${x} is greater than ${y}"
>       echo "   "
> fi

  5 is greater than 3
```

In the example above, **-lt** was as an operator to check for a "less than" condition, and **-eq** was used to check for an "equal" condition. Table 8.3 below contains a list of operators available for use when evaluating conditional statements:

Operator	Meaning	Mathematical Equivalent
-eq	equal to	$x == y$
-ge	greater than or equal to	$x >= y$
-gt	greater than	$x > y$
-le	less than or equal to	$x <= y$
-lt	less than	$x < y$
-ne	not equal to	$x != y$

Table 8.3: *Operators available for conditional statements and their meanings*

Next we will look at how we can use **test** to check for even more conditions.

Using the test Command or [expression]

Either the **test** command or just an expression in square brackets (**[expression]**) can be used to evaluate whether an expression is true (zero) or false (non-zero). As the following example illustrates, an expression evaluation can be accomplished in a number of different ways.

```
$ x=3
$ y=7
$ test $x -lt $y && echo " Option 1 --   ${x} is less than ${y} "
 Option 1 --   3 is less than 7
$ if test $x -lt $y
>   then
>     echo " Option 2 --   ${x} is less than ${y} "
> fi
 Option 2 --   3 is less than 7
$ if [ $x -lt $y ]
>   then
>     echo " Option 3 --   ${x} is less than ${y} "
> fi
 Option 3 --   3 is less than 7
```

The three conditional statements above all test for the exact same condition. In the first one, **&&** is used to execute the **echo** command if, and only if, the **exit status** of the **test** command is *0*.

The information in Table 8.4 below extracted from the Linux **man** page for **test** shows some of the other conditions we can **test** for. The information summarizes the different types of tests that can be performed on files:

Test	Description
-b	file exists and is block special
-c	file exists and is character special
-d	file exists and is a directory
-e	file exists
-f	file exists and is a regular file
-g	file exists and is set-group-ID
-G	file exists and is owned by the effective group ID
-h	file exists and is a symbolic link (same as -L
-k	file exists and has its sticky bit set
-L	file exists and is a symbolic link (same as -h)
-O	file exists and is owned by the effective user ID
-p	file exists and is a named pipe
-r	file exists and is readable
-S	file exists and is a socket
-s	file exists and has a size greater than zero
-t	file descriptor FD (stdout by default) is opened on a terminal
-u	file exists and its set-user-ID bit is set
-w	file exists and is writable
-x	file exists and is executable
-nt	file1 is newer (modification date) than file2
-ot	file1 is older than file2
-ef	file1 and file2 have the same device and inode numbers

Table 8.4: *Linux tests and their descriptions*

This type of test can be useful to check if your script relies on a certain file being around or writable for things to work right. The following are file test examples:

```
$ if [ -e ".bash_profile" ]
> then
>   echo " The file exists "
> else
>   echo " File not found "
> fi
 The file exists
```

```
$ if [ -e ".bash_proxxx" ]
> then
>   echo " The file exists "
> else
>   echo " File not found "
> fi
```

There are even more things we can test for when it comes to comparing strings. Table 8.5 contains string tests and their descriptions.

Test	Description
!=	the strings are not equal
=	the strings are equal
-l	evaluates to the length of the string
-n	the length of string is nonzero
-z	the length of string is zero

Table 8.5: *String tests and descriptions*

The following examples illustrate one use of the string **test**.

```
$ if [ -n "" ]
> then
>   echo " The string contains characters"
> else
>   echo " The string is empty "
> fi
 The string is empty
```

```
$ if [ -n "ABC  123" ]
> then
>   echo " The string contains characters"
> else
>   echo " The string is empty "
> fi
 The string contains characters
```

Any of these simple test conditions can be evaluated individually or combined with other conditions to evaluate complex expressions. Table 8.6 contains the connectives for test and their descriptions.

Connective	Description
!	expression is false
-a	both expression1 and expression2 are true (logical and)
-o	either expression1 or expression2 is true (logical or)

Table 8.6: *Connectives and their descriptions*

Here is how we could use the **or** connective to check two separate conditions:

```
$ a="abc"
$ b="abc"
$ if [ "$a" = "xyz" -o "$a" = "$b" ]
>   then
> echo "  One of the conditions is true "
>   else
> echo "  Neither condition is true "
> fi
  One of the conditions is true
$ a="abc"
$ b="xyz"
$ if [ "$a" = "xyz" -o "$a" = "$b" ]
>   then
> echo "  One of the conditions is true "
>   else
> echo "  Neither condition is true "
> fi
  Neither condition is true
```

Complex conditions can be used to evaluate several factors and react to certain conditions on the system or in the shell script. Next we'll see how these conditions can be used within loops to repeat an action.

Loops

A **loop** provides a way to execute commands repeatedly until a condition is satisfied. The bash shell provides several looping methods but we'll focus on the **for loop** and the **while loop**.

for loop

The **for loop** executes the commands placed between the **do** and **done** statements until all values in the value list passed to it have been processed. Here is a simple example of the **for loop**:

```
$ animals="dog cat bird mouse"
$
$ for animal in $animals
> do
>   echo $animal
> done
dog
```

```
cat
bird
mouse
```

As we can see here, we did not have to tell the **for** loop how many times to repeat. It just took the input and repeated it for the number of separate items in the variable *$animals*. It is easy to see how we might use this to parse over a list of filenames from the user.

while loop

The **while loop** executes the commands between the **do** and **done** statements while a given condition is true. The **while** loop must contain something which will eventually cause the condition to become false, otherwise an infinite loop would occur, and the commands would be executed forever. The following is an example of the use of a **while loop**:

```
$ a=2
$ i=1
$ while [ $i -le 20 ]
> do
>   echo "$a * $i = `expr $i \* $a`"
>   i=`expr $i + 1`
> done
2 * 1 = 2
2 * 2 = 4
2 * 3 = 6
2 * 4 = 8
2 * 5 = 10
2 * 6 = 12
2 * 7 = 14
2 * 8 = 16
2 * 9 = 18
2 * 10 = 20
2 * 11 = 22
2 * 12 = 24
2 * 13 = 26
2 * 14 = 28
2 * 15 = 30
2 * 16 = 32
2 * 17 = 34
2 * 18 = 36
2 * 19 = 38
2 * 20 = 40
```

Different loops are useful for different situations. A poorly written loop can wind up executing indefinitely and may fill your hard drive, use all your processor or cause you to run out of free memory. Beware the infinite loop!

The case Statement

Instead of nesting many **if-then-else** or **if-then-elif-then** statements, another alternative is to use the **case** statement. The **case** statement allows the user to perform a different set of commands depending upon the value associated with a string variable.

The following example shows use of the **case** statement as you might see it in a shell script:

```
echo -n " What type of pet do you have (dog, cat, etc.)? "
read pet
echo "  "
case $pet in
   dog)     echo " So you have a dog ..."
            echo " That's nice, so do I."
            echo " My dog's name is Fido.";;
   cat)     echo " So you have a cat ..."
            echo " I'm allergic to cats!";;
   fish)    echo " So you have fish ..."
            echo " Can't take them for a walk .. ha, ha.";;
   ferret)  echo " Ferrets are cool!";;
   *)       echo " A $pet ... that's a funny pet";;
esac
echo "  "
```

The **case** example script above asks the user what kind of pet they have and then provides different responses depending upon the type of pet answered. It looks for answers of "dog", "cat", "fish", "ferret", and "*****".

The asterisk (*****) matches any other answer supplied by the user. When a match is found by the case statement, all commands are executed until a double semi-colon (**;;**) is encountered.

When the example above is entered and saved to a file called **whatpet.sh**, it can be run as shown below:

```
$ /bin/bash ./whatpet.sh

What type of pet do you have (dog, cat, etc.)? moose

A moose ... that's a funny pet

$ ./whatpet.ksh

What type of pet do you have (dog, cat, etc.)? dog

So you have a dog ...
That's nice, so do I.
My dog's name is Fido.
```

Now that information has been presented on most of the scripting command constructs, it is possible to begin writing scripts. The following section lists commands that may be useful in creating scripts.

Linux Command Summary

The following is a fairly comprehensive list of commands available in the Red Hat distribution of Linux. A brief description of each command is presented in Table 8.7 below. Some of the commands have been presented in greater detail in previous chapters.

Rather than spend a great deal of time discussing each command in detail and giving examples of each, the commands are presented here only to give you an idea of what is available. If you find a command here that might be useful in the development of a script, you can learn more about it with the **man** or **info** tools. Many of the following descriptions come directly from the Linux **man** pages.

Command	Description
ac	**ac** prints out a report of connect time, in hours, based on the logins/logouts in the current **wtmp** file. A total is also printed out.
alias	**alias** with no arguments or with the **-p** option prints the list of aliases in the form **alias name=value** on standard output. When arguments are supplied, an alias is defined for each name whose value is given. A trailing space in value causes the next word to be checked for alias substitution when the alias is expanded. For each name in the argument list for which no value is supplied, the name and value of the alias is printed. **alias** returns true unless a name is given for which no alias has

Command	Description
	been defined.
at	**at** and **batch** read commands from standard input or a specified file which are to be executed at a later time. **at** executes commands at a specified time. **atq** lists the user's pending jobs, unless the user is the superuser; in that case, everybody's jobs are listed. The format of the output lines, one for each job,is: Job number; date;hour; and job class. **atrm** deletes jobs identified by their job number. **batch** executes commands when system load levels permit; in other words, when the load average drops below 0.8, or the value specified in the invocation of **atrun**.
awk	*Gawk* is the GNU Project's implementation of the *AWK* programming language. **Gawk** - pattern scanning and processing language
basename	Print **name** with any leading directory components removed. If specified, also remove a trailing **suffix**.
bc	**bc** is a calculator that supports arbitrary precision numbers with interactive execution of statements.
bg	Resume the suspended job **jobspec** in the background, as if it had been started with **&**.
break	Exit from within **a for**, **while**, **until**, or **select** loop regardless of the loop condition.
cal	**cal** displays a simple calendar. If arguments are not specified, the current month is displayed.
cancel	Cancel jobs
cat	Concatenate files and print on the standard output
chdir	chdir changes the current directory to that specified in path.
chfn	chfn is used to change finger information. This information is stored in the **/etc/passwd** file, and is displayed by the finger program.
chgrp	Change the group membership **files**.
chmod	Change file access permissions
chown	Change file owner and group
chsh	Change the user's login shell
cksum	Checksum and count the bytes in a file
clear	Clears the screen, if possible.
cmp	The **cmp** utility compares two files of any type and writes the results to the standard output.
col	Filter reverse line feeds from input
comm	Compare two sorted files line by line
compress	**compress**, **uncompress**, **zcat** - compress and expand data
continue	Resume the next iteration of the enclosing **for**, **while**, **until**, or **select** loop.
cp	Copy files and directories
cpio	Copy files to and from archives
crontab	Maintain **crontab** files for individual users

Command	Description
csplit	Split a file into sections determined by context lines
ctags	Generate tag files for source code
cut	Remove sections from each line of files
date	Print or set the system date and time
df	Report filesystem disk space usage
diff	Find differences between two files
du	Estimate file space usage
echo	Display a line of text
ed	**Ed** is a line-oriented text editor. It is used to create, display, modify and manipulate text files.
egrep	**Grep**, **egrep**, **fgrep** - print lines matching a pattern
emacs	Text editor
env	Run a program in a modified environment
exit	Cause the shell to exit
expand	Convert tabs in each **file** to spaces, writing to standard output.
expr	Evaluate and print the value of **expression** to standard output
false	Exit with a status code indicating failure.
fg	Resume job in the foreground, and make it the current job
fgrep	**Grep**, **egrep**, **fgrep** - print lines matching a pattern
file	Determine file type
find	Search for files in a directory hierarchy
finger	User information lookup program
fmt	Simple optimal text formatter
fold	Wrap each input line to fit in specified width
ftp	Basic file transfer program
getfacl	Get file access control lists
grep	**Grep**, **egrep**, **fgrep** - print lines matching a pattern
groupadd	Create a new group
groupdel	Delete a group
groupmod	Modify a group
gunzip	Expand compressed files
gzip	Compress files
halt	**halt**, **reboot**, **poweroff** - stop the system
hash	For each name, the full file name of the command is determined by searching the directories in $PATH and remembered
head	Output the first part of files
help	Display helpful information about builtin commands
history	Display recently executed commands
hostname	Show or set the system's host name
id	Print information for USERNAME, or the current user
ifconfig	Display or configure the kernel-resident network interfaces
jobs	Lists the active jobs
join	Join lines of two files on a common field. For each pair of input lines

Command	Description
	with identical join fields, write a line to standard output
kill	Terminate a process
ld	Linker. **ld** combines a number of object and archive files, relocates their data and ties up symbol references
ldd	Print shared library dependencies
less	**less** is a program similar to **more** , but it allows backward movement in the file as well as forward movement
lex	Used for pattern matching on text
ln	Make links between files
locate	Security Enhanced version of the GNU **locate**. It provides a secure way to index and quickly search for files on the system
login	**login** is used when signing onto a system. It can also be used to switch from one user to another at any time
logname	Print the name of the current user
logout	Exit a login shell
lp	Submits files for printing or alters a pending job
lpadmin	Configures printer and class queues provided by CUPS. It can also be used to set the server default printer or class.
lpc	Provides limited control over printer and class queues provided by CUPS. It can also be used to query the state of queues.
lpq	Shows the current print queue status on the named printer
lpr	Submits files for printing
lprm	Cancels print jobs that have been queued for printing
lpstat	Displays status information about the current classes, jobs, and printers
ls	List directory contents
mail	Send and receive mail
make	The purpose of the **make** utility is to determine automatically which pieces of a large program need to be recompiled and issue the commands to recompile them
man	Formats and displays the on-line manual pages
mesg	Controls the write access to the user's terminal by others
mkdir	Make directories
more	**more** is a filter for paging through text one screenful at a time
mount	Mount a file system
mt	Control magnetic tape drive operation
mv	Move or rename files
neqn	Format equations for ASCII output
netstat	Print network connections, routing tables, interface statistics, masquerade connections, and multicast memberships
newgrp	Log in to a new group
nice	Run a program with modified scheduling priority
nohup	Run a command immune to hangups, with output to a non-tty
nslookup	Query Internet name servers interactively

Command	Description
passwd	Update a user's authentication tokens(s)
paste	Merge lines of files. It write lines consisting of the sequentially corresponding lines from each **file**, separated by tabs, to standard output
perl	Practical Extraction and Report Language
pgrep	Looks through the currently running processes and lists the process ids which match the selection criteria to stdout
ping	Uses the ICMP protocol's mandatory **ECHO_REQUEST** datagram to elicit an ICMP **ECHO_RESPONSE** from a host or gateway
pkill	Will send the specified signal, by default SIGTERM, to each process instead of listing them on stdout
poweroff	Halt, reboot, poweroff - stop the system
pr	Paginate or columnate **file**(s) for printing
printf	Format and print data to the standard output
ps	Report process status
pwd	Print name of current/working directory
rcp	Remote file copy ... copies files between machines
reboot	Halt, reboot, poweroff - stop the system
red	**ed** is a line-oriented text editor. It is used to create, display, modify and otherwise manipulate text files. **red** is a restricted **ed**: it can only edit files in the current directory and cannot execute shell commands.
rlogin	Remote login
rm	Remove files or directories
rmail	Handle remote mail received via uucp
rmdir	Remove empty directories
rpcinfo	Report remote procedure call (RPC) information. It makes a RPC call to a RPC server and reports what it finds.
rsh	Remote shell
s2p	**Psed** - A stream editor that reads the input stream consisting of the specified files (or standard input, if none are given), processes it line by line by applying a script consisting of edit commands, and writes resulting lines to standard output.
sar	Collect, report, or save system activity information
script	Makes a typescript of everything printed on a terminal
sdiff	Find differences between two files and merge interactively
sed	A stream editor. A stream editor is used to perform basic text transformations on an input stream
sendmail	An electronic mail transport agent that sends a message to one or more recipients, routing the message over whatever networks are necessary
set	Display, set or unset shell attributes.
setenv	Change or add an environment variable
setfacl	Set file access control lists
sh	The bourne shell. **bash** is an bourne-compatible command language interpreter that executes commands read from the standard input or from

Command	Description
	a file.
shutdown	Brings the system down in a secure way. All logged-in users are notified that the system is going down, and **login** is blocked.
sleep	Delay for a specified amount of time or pause for *number* of seconds
sort	Sort lines of text files
split	Split a file into pieces
stty	Change and print terminal line settings
su	Change the effective user id and group id to that of another *user*
sudo	Execute a command as another user. It allows a permitted user to execute a command as the superuser or another user, as specified in the sudoers file
sysinfo	Returns information on overall system statistics
tail	Output the last part of files
tar	The **tar** archiving utility
tee	Read from standard input and write to standard output and files
telnet	The telnet command is used to communicate with another host using the TELNET protocol
time	Time a simple command or give resource usage
touch	Update the access and modification times of each **file** to the current time
tput	Initialize a terminal or query terminfo database
tr	Translate, squeeze, and/or delete characters from standard input, writing to standard output
traceroute	Print the route packets take to a network host
troff	The **troff** processor of the **groff** text formatting system
ul	Do underlining
umask	Set the user file-creation mask
unalias	Remove a named **alias** from the list of defined aliases
uname	Print certain system information
uncompress	Expand compressed data
uniq	Remove duplicate lines from a sorted file
useradd	Create a new user or update default new user information
userdel	Delete a user account and related files
usermod	Modify a user account
vi	A powerfull text editor.
view	Start the **vi** editor in read-only mode
wait	Wait for the specified process and return its termination status.
wc	Print byte, word, and newline counts for each **file**, and a total line if more than one **file** is specified.
whereis	Locate the binary, source, and manual page files for a command
which	Shows the full path of shell commands
who	Show who is logged on
whois	**whois** searches *Whois* servers for the named object.

Command	Description
X	The **X** Window System is a network transparent window system which runs on a wide range of computing and graphics machines
xfd	Display all the characters in an **X** font
xlsfonts	Server font list displayer for **X**
xrdb	**X** server resource database utility
xset	User preference utility for **X**
xterm	The **xterm** program is a terminal emulator for the **X** Window System
zcat	Compress or expand files

Conclusions

We started this chapter with a quick overview of Linux shell programming and tried it out with a simple script. We showed how an **alias** may be used instead of a shell script when only a command or two are needed, then we talked about how to view and set variables including those which are defined within the shell.

We then looked at how the shell can be used to do math. We used the **echo** command to try out some of the different ways of quoting things in Linux and saw how the results differ.

We spent some time looking at how to read the exit code of a command which will often tell us if the command was successful. How to accept information into a shell script through command line arguments was also covered.

We saw how to redirect output to a file and how a file can be used as input for a command and then saw how **pipes** can be used to redirect data between commands.

Conditions and loops were introduced and we talked about different conditions we can evaluate for. Finally we looked at some of the commands available within Linux just to get an idea of what is possible.

In the next chapter we'll look at how commands and shell scripts can be scheduled to run on a regular basis with the **cron** command.

Scheduling Jobs with crontab

Scheduled maintenance can keep a Linux server tidy

The cron Daemon

This final chapter will introduce the details on how to schedule shell scripts to execute on a regular timetable. The **cron** daemon is the system task that runs scripted jobs on a pre-determined schedule. The **crontab** command is used to tell the **cron** daemon what jobs the user wants to run and when to run those jobs.

Each Linux user can have their own **crontab** file, if allowed by the System Administrator. The administrator controls use of **crontab** by including users in the **cron.deny** file to disallow use of **crontab**.

crontab Options

As shown in Table 10.1, the **crontab** command has several options with different purposes.

Option	Purpose
-e	edit the current *crontab* file using the text editor specified by the *EDITOR* environment variable or the *VISUAL* environment variable
-l	list the current *crontab* file
-r	remove the current *crontab* file
-u	specifies the user's *crontab* to be manipulated. This is usually used by *root* to manipulate the *crontab* of other users or can be used by you to correctly identify the *crontab* to be manipulated if you have used the *su* command to assume another identity.

Table 10.1: *crontab options and purposes*

crontab also accepts a file name and will use the specified file to create the **crontab** file. Many users prefer to use this option rather than the **crontab -e** command because it provides a master file from which the **crontab** is built, thus providing a backup to the **crontab**. The following example specifies a file called **mycron.tab** to be used as the input for **crontab**.

```
$ crontab mycron.tab
```

Here's how you would use the **crontab -l** command to view the current **cron** entries for the logged in user.

```
$ crontab -l

#***************************************************************
# Run the Weekly file cleanup task at 6:00AM every Monday
# and send any output to a file called cleanup.lst in the
# /tmp directory
#***************************************************************
```

```
00 06 * * 1 /home/terry/cleanup.ksh > /tmp/cleanup.lst


#*************************************************************
# Run the Weekly Management Report every Monday at 7:00 AM
# and save a copy of the report in my /home directory
#*************************************************************
00 07 * * 1 /home/terry/weekly_mgmt_rpt.ksh wprd >
/home/terry/weekly_mgmt_rpt.lst
```

Now if we wanted to delete all the entries in the crontab we can use the **–r** option.

```
$ crontab -r
```

The Format of the crontab File

The **crontab** file consists of a series of entries specifying what shell scripts to run and when to run it. It is also possible to document **crontab** entries with comments. Lines which have a pound sign (**#**) as the first non-blank character are considered comments. Blank lines are completely ignored. Comments cannot be specified on the same line as **cron** command lines. Comments must be kept on their own lines within the **crontab**.

There are two types of command lines that can be specified in the **crontab**: environment variable settings and **cron** commands. The following sections will provide more detail on these two types of crontab entries.

Environment variable settings

Each environment variable line consists of a variable name, an equal sign (**=**), and a value. Values that contain spaces need to be enclosed within quotes. The following are some examples of environment variable settings:

```
color = red
title = 'My Life in a Nutshell'
```

It is important to remember that variable names are case sensitive and that system variables are usually defined with upper case names, while user defined variables are defined with lower case names.

crontab Command Lines

Each **crontab** command line is comprised of six positional fields specifying the time, date and shell script or command to be run. The format of the **crontab** command line is described in Table 10.2 below:

Field	Minute	Hour	Day of Month	Month	Day of Week	Command
Valid values	0-59	0-23	1-31	1-12	0-7	Command path/command

Table 10.2: *crontab command line format*

Each of these fields can contain a single number, a range of numbers indicated with a hyphen (such as **2-4**), a list of specific values separated by commas (like **2,3,4**) or a combination of these designations separated by commas (such as **1,3-5**). Any of these fields may also contain an asterisk (*****) indicating every possible value of this field. This can all get rather confusing so let's take a look at a few examples.

The next several examples are all part of the same **crontab** file. We have broken it up in order to explain each entry individually.

```
# Use the Korn Shell for all shell scripts
SHELL=/bin/ksh
```

This sets the default shell for these cron scripts by setting the *SHELL* environment variable.

```
#*************************************************************
# Run the Weekly file cleanup task at 6:00AM every Monday
# and send any output to a file called cleanup.lst in the
# /tmp directory
#*************************************************************
00 06 * * 1 /home/terry/cleanup.ksh > /tmp/cleanup.lst
```

This entry will run the script **cleanup.ksh** at 0 minutes past the hour, 6 am, every day of the month, every month of the year, but only on Mondays. This illustrates that for a crontab to execute *all* of the conditions specified must be met, so even though we've said *every day of the month* by making the third field a wildcard, the day also has to meet the final condition that the day is a *Monday*.

```
#************************************************************
# Run the Weekly Management Report every Monday at 7:00 AM
# and save a copy of the report in my /home directory
#************************************************************
00 07 * * 1 /home/terry/weekly_mgmt_rpt.ksh wprd >
/home/terry/weekly_mgmt_rpt.lst
```

This entry is very similar but will execute at 7:00am. Since the hour is in 24 hour format (midnight is actually represented as **00**) we know the **07** represents 7:00 a.m. This entry again will only be run once a week.

```
#************************************************************
# Weekly Full Backup - run every Sunday at 1:30AM
#************************************************************
30 01 * * 0 /home/terry/full_backup.ksh wprd > /tmp/full_backup.lst
```

Here we have specified this script to be run at **30** minutes past the hour, the *first* hour of the day, but only on Sundays. Remember that in the day of the week column Sunday can be represented by either **0** or **7**.

```
#************************************************************
# Nightly Incremental Backup - run Monday-Saturday at 1:30AM
#************************************************************
30 01 * * 1-6 /home/terry/incr_backup.ksh  > /tmp/incr_backup.lst
```

In this **crontab** entry we see the same indication for hour and minute as the last entry but we have specified a range for the day of the week. The range **1-6** will cause the incr_backup.ksh to be executed at 1:30 every morning from Monday through Saturday.

```
#************************************************************
# Low disk space alert ... run every 15 minutes, sending
# alerts to key individuals via e-mail
#************************************************************
00,15,30,45 * * * * /home/terry/free_space.ksh > /tmp/free_space.lst
```

This entry has minutes separated by a comma indicating that it should be run at each of the indicated times. Since all the other fields are wildcards (*****) the entry will be run on the hour (**00**), **15** minutes past the hour, **30** minutes past the hour and **45** minutes past the hour.

```
#*************************************************************
# Lunch Time Notification - run Monday-Friday at Noon -
# sends a message to all users indicating it's lunch time
#*************************************************************
00 12 * * 1-5 /home/terry/lunch_time.ksh wprd > /tmp/lunch_time.lst
```

This lunch reminder is set up to run at 12:00 p.m. Monday through Friday only.

The most important thing to remember is that a **crontab** entry will execute every time all of its conditions are met. To take the last entry as an example, any time it is **00** minutes past the hour of **12** on any day of the month and any month of the year and the day of the week is between Monday and Friday inclusive (**1-5**) this crontab will be executed.

You will use wildcards in most **crontab** entries but be careful where you use them. For instance, if we mistakenly placed a ***** in the minute position of the last crontab example above we would end up running the script for *ever* minute of the 12:00 hour instead of just once at the beginning of the hour. I don't think anyone needs that many reminders to go to lunch, do you?

As mentioned above, the **day-of-week** field accepts either zero or seven as a value for Sunday. Any of the time/date fields can also contain an asterisk (*****) indicating the entire range of values. Additionally, **month** and **day-of-week** fields can contain name values, consisting of the first three letters of the month, as indicated in Table 10.3 below.

Field	Valid Entries (case insensitive)
Days of the week	sun, mon, tue, wed, thu, fri, sat SUN, MON, TUE, WED, THU, FRI, SAT
Months of	jan, feb, mar, apr, may, jun, jul, aug, sep, oct, nov, dec

year	JAN, FEB, MAR, APR, MAY, JUN, JUL, AUG, SEP, OCT, NOV, DEC

Table 10.3: *day-of-week field values*

When numbers are used, the user can specify a range of values separated by a hyphen or a list of values separated by commas. In other words, specifying 2-5 in the hour field means 2AM, 3AM, 4AM and 5AM, while specifying 2,5 means only 2AM and 5AM.

We've talked an awful lot about how to specify the date and time in the **crontab** but what about the command? Well, most folks will write shell scripts to execute with their **crontab** entries but you can actually just execute a command from the crontab as well. Either way make sure you put the **absolute path** to your command in the crontab.

If the command or script you call in your **crontab** typically sends output to the screen you will probably want to redirect that output to a log file with the **>>** symbol so you can check it later. Be careful with this as the log files may get rather large over time!

Conclusions

In this chapter, we covered how to schedule commands and shell scripts to run at certain times of day, on certain days of the week, or days of the month, etc. This allows the automation of processes that need to be run repetitively on a fixed schedule.

With careful setup and scheduling you will find you can automate most repetitive tasks with a combination of shell scripting and the use of **cron**. This can save you hours a day on a large or complex system!

Now we'll look at some Linux administration commands which can be used to setup and maintain the overall system.

Linux Administrator Commands

Even if you are not the system administrator for the Linux box you use it will often be necessary to perform some basic administrative commands throughout the workday. Some of the commands require being logged into the system as the root user.

In Linux, the root user is the administrator user with complete authority on that system. The root user is created when the operating system is installed and is the most powerful user on any Linux system; thus, the root user has the authority to do whatever, whenever.

Because of its power most administrators will not hand out the root user on a production machine and rightly so! If you are given the root password, be very careful. You could easily delete other user's files, kill their running programs or completely destroy the entire server.

Since the root user has so much power many administrators give limited administrative privileges to users using a command called **sudo** (typically pronounced like "pseudo".) Through the use of **sudo** the administrator can allow you to run only certain commands as root and can track what you have executed.

If you have been given **sudo** access to run a command as root all you have to do is prefix the command you want to run with **sudo** like this:

```
$ sudo shutdown -r +3
```

Shutting Down and Changing Runlevels

On occasion, it may be necessary to shut down the Linux server or reboot it after a configuration change. The execution of the shutdown command requires root privileges. After all, it would not be good to have just anyone shutting down a server, particularly a production server running critical business applications.

When the shutdown command is issued, all users that are directly logged in are notified that the system is going down and further logins are disabled. The administrator has the option of shutting down the system immediately or after a delayed warning period. If there are other users on the system, the courteous thing to do would be to warn them that the system is being shut down so that they can save their work and log off the system gracefully.

Always keep in mind that people may be using a system through a web page or other indirect means. These people will not receive any warning when the system is shut down.

To shutdown a server immediately we specify **now** as the time. The **–h** option causes the system to be halted after the shutdown.

```
$ shutdown -h now
```

The **–r** option here is used to cause the system to reboot after it has shutdown. As mentioned above, if other users are currently on the system it would be nice to give them a little warning so here we have specified **+3** to cause the system to warn users and wait three minutes before restarting.

```
$ shutdown -r +3
```

Yet another form of the **shutdown** command will allow you to specify the time which you want the command to happen.

```
$ shutdown -r 17:00
```

The command above will cause the system to reboot at 5:00 p.m.

The state or mode of a Linux system is described as a **runlevel**. The **shudtown** command is one way to control what runlevel a Linux system is running in. For instance, **shutdown –h now** seen above will change the runlevel to 0 and **shutdown −r +3** will change the runlevel to 6. The runlevels control what can be run on a system and who can log into it.

If the system is running and you would like to change the runlevel, for instance if you need to do some maintenance in single user mode, you can use the **telinit** command to change the current runlevel.

```
# telinit 1
```

While you can use **telinit** to switch to a higher or lower runlevel changing to a lower runlevel may sometimes have unexpected results and will definitely kick others off the system. Use it with care.

When the system boots it will come up to the specified runlevel (runlevel 5 by default.) Certain things are enabled at each runlevel and specific scripts will be run as the system enters a runlevel. Typically a running Linux system will be in runlevel 5.

Let's take a quick look at each of the runlevels.

- 0: Used to halt the system

- 1: Single-user mode for performing administrative tasks

- 2: Multi-user mode, without networking

- 3: Multi-user mode, with networking

- 4: Currently unused

- 5: Multi-user mode with graphical user interface (GUI), usually the default runlevel

- 6: Used to reboot the system

To find out what runlevel you are currently running in you can use the **−r** option of the **who** command.

```
$ who -r
         run-level 5  Oct  4 20:08                    last=S
```

Later on we'll use the **who** command to look at who is on the system.

While it is possible in some versions of Linux to go from a higher to a lower runlevel without rebooting it can occasionally cause problems. Often it is easier to get to a lower runlevel via restart.

Adding and Removing Users

While some Linux systems only have a couple active users others can have dozens or even hundreds. Most Linux systems offer a graphical interface for managing users but you should also know how to add and remove users from the command line. You will need root privileges to add users.

A user can be added to Linux with the **useradd** command. This will create an entry for the user in the /etc/passwd and /etc/shadow files and create that users home directory in the default home location.

```
# useradd chuck
```

Now that the user has been created we should assign a password to them so they can log in. The **passwd** command can be used to change a user's password. If you're logged in as root you can call the **passwd** command with a user's name as an argument to change the password of another user.

```
# passwd chuck
Changing password for user chuck.
New UNIX password: pencil1983
Retype new UNIX password: pencil1983
passwd: all authentication tokens updated successfully.
```

Now we can let this user know that his account is ready and give him his password. There are several other options for the **useradd** command which we have not covered here, but this is enough to add a basic user.

Of course on the other end of things you will occasionally need to remove a user from the system. We can do that with the **userdel** command. The **userdel** command can be used with the **–r** option to automatically delete the user's home directory. Just make sure if you are using the **–r** option that there is nothing in the user's home directory that you need!

```
# ls ~chuck
# userdel -r chuck
```

Here we have listed the user's home directory and it is empty. Actually there are some hidden files which were created with the home directory but we are not concerned about them. Next we use the **userdel –r** command to remove the user and their home directory.

Get Process Status

To view the current processes (running programs) active within the system, the process status (**ps**) command can be used. The **ps** command accepts a large number of options; however, the most useful ones are the show all (**–e**) option and the show full (**–f**) option, which can be entered as follows:

```
$ ps -ef
UID        PID  PPID  C STIME TTY        TIME CMD
terry     3696 18588  0 18:10 ?      00:00:01 gnome-session
terry     4054     1  0 18:10 ?      00:00:01 /usr/lib/gconfd-2 11
terry    25812     1  0 18:10 ?      00:00:00 /usr/lib/bonobo-activation-serve
terry    11467     1  0 18:10 ?      00:00:00 gnome-smproxy --sm-client-id def
terry    13021     1  0 18:10 ?      00:00:00 gnome-settings-daemon --oaf-acti
terry     1519     1  0 18:10 ?      00:00:00 xscreensaver -nosplash
terry     4029     1  0 18:10 ?      00:00:11 /usr/bin/metacity --sm-client-id
terry    21462     1  0 18:10 ?      00:00:11 gnome-panel --sm-client-id defau
terry     2216 25609  0 18:10 ?      00:00:00 nautilus --no-default-window --s
terry    18785     1  0 18:10 ?      00:00:00 /usr/lib/notification-area-apple
terry    30999     1  0 18:10 ?      00:00:00 pam-panel-icon --sm-client-id de
terry     8494     1  0 18:55 ?      00:00:13 kwrite
terry     4890     1  0 18:55 ?      00:00:00 kdeinit: Running...
terry    16796     1  0 18:55 ?      00:00:00 kdeinit: dcopserver --nosid --su
terry    29590     1  0 18:55 ?      00:00:00 kdeinit: klauncher
terry     6513     1  0 18:55 ?      00:00:01 kdeinit: kded
terry    23583  4890  0 20:37 ?      00:00:00 kdeinit: kio_file file /tmp/ksoc
terry    21234     1 21 20:55 ?      00:00:01 /usr/bin/gnome-terminal
terry    17263 21234  0 20:55 ?      00:00:00 [gnome-pty-helpe]
terry    14241 21234  2 20:55 pts/0  00:00:00 bash
terry    18504 14241  0 20:55 pts/0  00:00:00 ps -ef
...
```

The command **ps –ef** will output lots of information about all the running commands on the system. Here's a quick explanation of what this output means:

Column	Description
UID	Username of the process owner
PID	Process ID number of this process
PPID	Process ID of the process which started this one (parent)
C	CPU utilization of this process
STIME	Start time (listed as month and day if older than 1 day)
TTY	The terminal (if any) the process was started from
TIME	The amount of CPU time this process has consumed
CMD	The command which was executed (long commands are truncated)

To see how processes are related in a hierarchical structured display, the **H** option can be added to the command as shown below:

```
$ s -efH
UID        PID  PPID C STIME TTY          TIME CMD
terry     3696 18588 0 18:10 ?        00:00:01 gnome-session
terry    21234     1 1 20:55 ?        00:00:08 /usr/bin/gnome-terminal
terry    17263 21234 0 20:55 ?        00:00:00   [gnome-pty-helpe]
terry    14241 21234 0 20:55 pts/0    00:00:00   bash
terry     4786 14241 0 21:05 pts/0    00:00:00     ps -efH
terry    31992 25609 0 18:10 ?        00:00:00       nautilus --no-default-window --sm-clien
terry    11456 25609 0 18:10 ?        00:00:01       nautilus --no-default-window --sm-clien
terry     2216 25609 0 18:10 ?        00:00:00       nautilus --no-default-window --sm-clien
terry    21462     1 0 18:10 ?        00:00:11 gnome-panel --sm-client-id default2
terry     4029     1 0 18:10 ?        00:00:14 /usr/bin/metacity --sm-client-id=default1
terry    13021     1 0 18:10 ?        00:00:00 gnome-settings-daemon --oaf-activate-iid=OA
terry    11467     1 0 18:10 ?        00:00:00 gnome-smproxy --sm-client-id default0
terry    25812     1 0 18:10 ?        00:00:00 /usr/lib/bonobo-activation-server --ac-acti
terry     4054     1 0 18:10 ?        00:00:01 /usr/lib/gconfd-2 11
```

This format makes it easy to track which processes created which by listing child processes directly below their parent and indenting the CMD output two spaces for child processes. In this example we see that process 21234 created two child processes, 17263 and 14241. It is easy to identify these as sibling processes as they are indented the same amount and both follow the same parent process. A quick check of the PPID confirms this.

In these examples we have been using the **ps** command to displays processes owned by all users with the **–e** option. This is often more than we need so we can instead use the **–u** option to show processes owned by a specific user. The following display is for the **lp** user:

```
$ ps -u lp
  PID TTY          TIME CMD
22233 ?        00:00:07 foomatic-rip
28688 ?        00:00:00 foomatic-rip
```

```
30970 ?        00:00:00 foomatic-rip
 7593 ?        00:00:00 sh
10833 ?        00:00:00 sh
 2005 ?        00:00:00 perl
32267 ?        00:00:03 gs
26226 ?        00:00:00 sh
 6930 ?        00:00:00 cat
```

Next we'll take a look at some other commands to gather information about running processes.

Find Processes by Pattern or User

The **pgrep** command is used to find processes which have a certain pattern in the command. The following command looks for processes containing the pattern **nautilus**. The process ID number of any matching process(es) is returned.

```
$ pgrep nautilus
18094
3149
20224
11597
31355
```

pgrep is a useful way to find specific running programs but should be used judiciously. You could very easily end up with more than you had planned.

Another way to see only those processes owned by a specific user is the **−u** option. The following are the *pid*s for the **lp** user:

```
$ pgrep −u lp
22233
28688
30970
7593
10833
2005
32267
26226
```

You can combine these two methods to match a specific user and pattern. Here we see the process IDs for processes owned by the user **lp** which match the pattern **foomatic**.

```
$ pgrep -u lp foomatic
22233
28688
30970
```

Now let's look at the most active processes in the system.

Display the Most Active Processes

The **top** command provides a dynamic display of the current activity within a Linux system. By default **top** will list running processes owned by all users. The processes which are currently using the most CPU are listed first and **top** will list as many processes as will fit on the screen.

```
$ top
top - 22:58:28 up  4:49,  2 users,  load average: 0.03, 0.08, 0.05
Tasks:  79 total,   1 running,  78 sleeping,   0 stopped,   0 zombie
Cpu(s):  22.3% user,   5.6% system,   0.0% nice,  72.1% idle
Mem:    255656k total,   238208k used,    17448k free,    23460k buffers
Swap:   506008k total,        0k used,   506008k free,    96400k cached

  PID USER      PR  NI  VIRT  RES  SHR S %CPU %MEM    TIME+  Command
18325 root      17   0 41524  16m 1952 S 23.6  6.5  5:10.99 X
21234 terry     12   0 10648  10m 7180 S  2.6  4.2  0:33.20 gnome-terminal
11784 root      14   0   984  984  772 R  1.6  0.4  0:00.46 top
    1 root       9   0   500  500  448 S  0.0  0.2  0:05.12 init
    2 root       9   0     0    0    0 S  0.0  0.0  0:00.06 keventd
    3 root       9   0     0    0    0 S  0.0  0.0  0:00.15 kapmd
    4 root      18  19     0    0    0 S  0.0  0.0  0:00.00 ksoftirqd_CPU0
    5 root       9   0     0    0    0 S  0.0  0.0  0:00.00 kswapd
    6 root       9   0     0    0    0 S  0.0  0.0  0:00.00 bdflush
    7 root       9   0     0    0    0 S  0.0  0.0  0:00.14 kupdated
    8 root      -1 -20     0    0    0 S  0.0  0.0  0:00.00 mdrecoveryd
   12 root       9   0     0    0    0 S  0.0  0.0  0:00.33 kjournald
13282 root       9   0     0    0    0 S  0.0  0.0  0:00.00 khubd
14301 root       9   0     0    0    0 S  0.0  0.0  0:00.00 kjournald
 8235 root       9   0   968  968  696 S  0.0  0.4  0:00.00 dhclient
13016 rpc        9   0   536  536  464 S  0.0  0.2  0:00.01 portmap
 1867 root       9   0   624  624  520 S  0.0  0.2  0:00.25 syslogd
 9038 root       9   0  1312 1312  436 S  0.0  0.5  0:00.32 klogd
27920 xfs        9   0  3724 3724  952 S  0.0  1.5  0:00.25 xfs
 4918 root       9   0  3096 3096 2952 S  0.0  1.2  0:00.18 gdm-binary
31982 daemon     9   0   504  504  444 S  0.0  0.2  0:00.00 atd
14666 root       9   0  1360 1360 1148 S  0.0  0.5  0:00.14 sshd
14744 root       9   0   876  876  756 S  0.0  0.3  0:00.02 xinetd
18588 root       9   0  4160 4160 3728 S  0.0  1.6  0:00.84 gdm-binary
22969 root       9   0  2040 2040 1296 S  0.0  0.8  0:01.08 cupsd
24020 lp         9   0  4232 4232 3756 S  0.0  1.7  0:07.72 foomatic-rip
22081 root       9   0  2332 2332 1164 S  0.0  0.9  0:00.58 smb
17197 root       9   0   452  452  416 S  0.0  0.2  0:00.00 rwhod
29921 root       9   0   552  552  508 S  0.0  0.2  0:00.07 rwhod
27808 lp         9   0  4236 4236 4056 S  0.0  1.7  0:00.01 foomatic-rip
```

Once you are done in **top** you just need to type **q** to quit and return to the command line.

Here we see the default **top** output. There's a lot here, but here are a few of the highlights. Some of this will be familiar from the **ps** output.

top output field	Description
up	How long this system has been running. May be in days
users	Number of connected users
load average	Number of processes currently running plus the number waiting to run over one, five and fifteen minutes*.
Tasks (or processes)	The total number of active processes
CPU	How the CPU is currently being used
user	The percent of CPU consumed by user processes
system	The percent of CPU consumed by system processes
idle	The percent of CPU not currently being used
iowait (not shown)	The percent of CPU spent waiting for data (typically disk)
Mem	Memory usage information
total	The total amount of memory in this system
used	Memory currently used in the system
free	Unused memory
Swap	Information about disk being used as memory
total	Total amount of disk assigned for use as memory
used	Swap currently in use
free	Unused swap
PID	Process ID number of this process
USER	Username of the process owner
%CPU	Percent of CPU currently being used by this process
%MEM	Percent of total memory being used by this process
TIME	Total CPU time consumed by this process
Command	The command which was executed (truncated)

* The calculation is more complicated than this, but this simple explanation will suffice for now. Generally a system with a load average lower than its number of CPUs is keeping up with its work. One with a load average of one to two times its number of CPUs is starting to fall behind and things aren't getting done as quickly as they are coming in, but a load average of several times the number of CPUs typically indicates the system is bogged down. Of course user experience is the best indicator of system performance.

The one, five and fifteen minute load averages are useful for identifying the trend of the system. If the one minute load average is lower than the five and fifteen minute averages the system has probably finished some large tasks and the system is getting less busy than it previously was. If the one and five minute averages are higher it is likely the system is getting busier than it was fifteen minutes ago.

While running **top** there are several commands which will change what top shows you. Some common ones are:

- Spacebar: Refreshes the display

- **h**: Display the help screen

- **k**: Kills a process*

- **n**: Changes the number of processes displayed

- **u**: Specify what user's tasks to view (blank for all users)

- **p**: Sorts tasks by CPU usage

- **s**: Change the number of seconds between refreshing

- **q**: Quit **top**

*We'll talk more about killing processes later in this chapter. For now you probably don't want to use this command. The rest of them you can go ahead and experiment with.

As with most other commands, **top** can be started with a number of different options. The most commonly used option when logged in as root is the **-u** option to limit the active process display to a particular user.

```
$ top -u terry
top - 23:20:22 up  5:11,  2 users,  load average: 0.33, 0.17, 0.06
Tasks:  79 total,   2 running,  77 sleeping,   0 stopped,   0 zombie
Cpu(s):  18.8% user,   4.2% system,   0.0% nice,  77.0% idle
Mem:    255656k total,   240748k used,    14908k free,    24772k buffers
Swap:   506008k total,        0k used,   506008k free,    96796k cached

  PID USER      PR  NI  VIRT  RES  SHR S %CPU %MEM    TIME+  Command
21462 terry      9   0 12440  12m 8332 S  2.4  4.9   0:15.11 gnome-panel --sm-client-id
default2
21234 terry      9   0 12380  12m 8160 S  1.8  4.8   0:47.21 /usr/bin/gnome-terminal
 4029 terry      9   0  7476 7476 5040 S  1.4  2.9   0:30.15 /usr/bin/metacity --sm-client-
id=default1
 7416 terry      9   0 27600  26m  10m S  1.0 10.8   0:32.55 nautilus --no-default-window -
-sm-client-id default3
 6513 terry      9   0 11736  11m  10m S  0.2  4.6   0:02.20 kdeinit: kded
 3696 terry      9   0  8724 8720 5876 S  0.0  3.4   0:01.79 gnome-session
 4054 terry      9   0  7224 7224 1988 S  0.0  2.8   0:01.79 /usr/lib/gconfd-2 11
```

```
25812 terry      9    0  2472 2472 1904 S   0.0   1.0   0:00.39 /usr/lib/bonobo-activation-
server --ac-activate --ior-output-f
11467 terry      9    0  2676 2676 2148 S   0.0   1.0   0:00.88 gnome-smproxy --sm-client-id
default0
13021 terry      9    0  6420 6416 5092 S   0.0   2.5   0:00.97 gnome-settings-daemon --oaf-
activate-iid=OAFIID:GNOME_Settings
11135 terry      9    0  1744 1744 1140 S   0.0   0.7   0:06.07 [fam]
25609 terry      9    0 27600  26m  10m S   0.0  10.8   0:00.19 nautilus --no-default-window -
-sm-client-id default3
31992 terry      9    0 27600  26m  10m S   0.0  10.8   0:00.58 nautilus --no-default-window -
-sm-client-id default3
11456 terry      9    0 27600  26m  10m S   0.0  10.8   0:01.55 nautilus --no-default-window -
-sm-client-id default3
 2216 terry      9    0 27600  26m  10m S   0.0  10.8   0:00.00 nautilus --no-default-window -
-sm-client-id default3
18785 terry      9    0  6920 6916 5604 S   0.0   2.7   0:00.69 /usr/lib/notification-area-
applet --oaf-activate-iid=OAFIID:GN
30999 terry      9    0  4228 4228 3508 S   0.0   1.7   0:01.08 pam-panel-icon --sm-client-id
default4
 8494 terry      9    0 17724  17m  13m S   0.0   6.9   0:30.34 kwrite
 4890 terry      8    0  7888 7888 7684 S   0.0   3.1   0:00.03 kdeinit: Running...
16796 terry      9    0  8380 8380 8080 S   0.0   3.3   0:00.08 kdeinit: dcopserver --nosid --
suicide
29590 terry      9    0  8924 8924 8540 S   0.0   3.5   0:00.21 kdeinit: klauncher
23583 terry      9    0  8524 8524 8188 S   0.0   3.3   0:00.23 kdeinit: kio_file file
/tmp/ksocket-terry/klauncherjEhebb.slav
17263 terry      9    0   576  576  504 S   0.0   0.2   0:00.02 [gnome-pty-helpe]
14241 terry      9    0  1540 1540 1096 S   0.0   0.6   0:00.28 bash
```

Here we see the top processes owned by the user terry. As you can see, the **–u** option works very similarly with **top** as it did with **ps**.

While you are running **top** you can

Now that we know how to track down running processes we might find some we need to do away with. In the next section we'll see how to kill processes. Be careful with these commands, especially if you have root privileges!

Kill a Process

When good processes go bad it is often necessary to terminate them. The **kill** command is used to send a termination signal to the specified process or group. The default termination signal is a SIGTERM (15) signal. A process which receives a SIGTERM may be programmed to trap signals and perform specific functions or ignore the signal entirely.

kill takes a process ID as a parameter. The process ID can be found using any of the methods described earlier in this chapter.

The following example shows the xscreensaver process (2609) which is to be terminated.

```
$ pgrep xscreen
2609
$ kill 2609
```

Though we use **pgrep** to find the PID of this process here we could have also used a PID from the output of **top** or **ps**.

When there a stubborn process trapping the **kill** command and refusing to terminate, the **-9** (SIGKILL) signal should be used to kill the process. The -9 signal cannot be trapped by a process and ignored. If the xscreensaver process did not terminate after the last **kill** command, the new **kill** command would look like the following:

```
$ kill -9 2609
```

While the **kill** command is typically available to all users you will only be able to kill processes you own. To kill processes owned by other users you will need root privileges.

Kill Processes Using a Pattern

Rather than scanning through process ID (*PID*) numbers, it might be easier to kill a process or group of processes by searching for a pattern in the command name field. The **pkill** command is one way to accomplish this, as shown below. **pkill** matches processes in the same way pgrep does. Be very careful when using **pkill** as you could easily kill more than you wanted to!

Here we want to kill all processes called **xscreen**. First we use **pgrep** to make sure we get a reasonable number of PIDs back, then we kill the process with **pkill**.

```
$ pgrep xscreen
2609
$ pkill xscreen
```

Again, be careful using **pkill**, especially as root!

Kill All Processes Owned By a Particular User

The **pkill** command also recognizes the **–u** option to look only at a specific user's processes. By adding the **-u** option to the **pkill** command, it is possible to terminate any and all processes for the specified user. If, for example, the following command was entered by user **terry**, all **terry**'s active processes would be cancelled, and **terry** would be kicked off the system.

```
$ pkill -9 -u terry
```

 Please save any work in progress before trying this!

Since you have the ability to kill any user's processes this would be a quick way to stop everything they're doing. Be careful though, doing so may not make you any friends, if you know what I mean.

We've talked mostly about two users so far, root and you (terry in most of the examples,) but there could be more people than that on our Linux system! Next we'll look at how to tell who's logged in.

Logged In User Information

To get a quick count of how many users are on the system we can use the **uptime** command.

```
$ uptime
22:41:39 up  2:33,  2 users,  load average: 0.00, 0.00, 0.00
```

We also see some other useful information here, like the current system time, the amount of time since last startup and the load average. The load average here is exactly the same as we saw in the **top** command we looked at earlier.

For more detailed information about each logged in user, the **w** command can be used. The **w** command also shows the same information **uptime** did.

```
$ w
 22:42:14 up  2:34,  2 users,  load average: 0.00, 0.00, 0.00
USER     TTY       LOGIN@   IDLE   JCPU   PCPU WHAT
terry    :0        20:10    ?xdm?  5:24   1.49s gnome-session
terry    pts/1     22:22    0.00s  0.24s  0.04s /usr/sbin/sshd
```

Here we see the user name, what terminal they are connected through (TTY), when they logged in (LOGIN@), how long since they last did something (IDLE), the amount of CPU time used by all this session's processes (JCPU), the amount used by the current process (PCPU) and what the user is currently executing (WHAT).

who is another command which can be used to show who is logged on the system. It provides a bit less detail than **w**.

```
$ who
terry    :0            Oct  4 20:10
terry    pts/1         Oct  4 22:22 (172.16.10.102)
```

The **who** command does tell us where the user has connected from which may be useful. It may show an IP address as above or a hostname.

To also see the *PID* of each logged on user, the **-u** option can be added to the **who** command.

```
$ who -u
terry    :0            Oct  4 20:10  ?        20237
terry    pts/1         Oct  4 22:22  .         4176 (172.16.10.102)
```

The process ID for the user's main session is now shown as the second to last column.

Who Am I?

Sometimes it is useful to check who we are currently logged in as. To do that we use the **whoami** command.

```
$ whoami
terry
```

As you can see, the **whoami** command just returns the username of who we're logged in as. This becomes invaluable when we start switching users like we'll see in the next section.

Switch to a Different User

It is often necessary to switch from one user identity to another. For instance, the administrator may want to switch from a regular user login to the root logon in order to set up a new directory structure. In this example, the user's regular user login ID is terry. Instead of logging off as terry and then logging on as root, the **su** (substitute user) command facilitates an easy switch.

```
$ whoami
terry
$ su
Password: rootpassword
# whoami
root
# exit
$ whoami
terry
```

Here we use the **whoami** command to show that we're currently logged in as terry, and then we use the su command to temporarily become root. When we're done working as root we type **exit** to exit root's shell and go back to being terry. You may also notice the prompt changed from a $ to a #. This may not always be the case, but it's a good hint that if your prompt is a # you are probably running as root.

As with other commands, the **su** command has a number of available options, but one of the most useful ones is the - option. This option essentially logs the user into a new shell as the specified user with the specified user's profile. Another helpful option is the **-c** option which allows the user that is logged in to run a single command as the specified user. Without using the − option, the current profile is maintained when switching users and the environment variables, such as *path* for locating executables, remain unchanged.

Unless you are logged in as root, the system will ask for a password when an attempt to switch users is made. As root you can **su** at will and assume the identity of any user on the system. This is another reason you don't want just anybody having the root password.

Conclusions

In this chapter we covered some of the basic administration commands which are useful in Linux including commands to do the following:

- Execute commands as the root user by using **sudo** if it is available

- Shutdown or restart a Linux server

- View and change the current runlevel

- Add and remove users

- Get information on running processes including the most active processes

- Kill processes, one at a time or by matching patterns

- Show information on currently logged in users

- Check what user we're running as

- Become another user, including root, to run commands with other permissions

Many of these functions must be done as the root user. Because of its broad access the root user's password must be tightly protected.

Well, that's an awful lot for one chapter! In the next chapter, the focus will be diverted to some commands that detail with the hardware configuration of the Linux server.

Monitoring Memory and Processor

Linux Hardware

At times, the need will arise to determine some information about the hardware components on the Linux system or check some of the parameter settings that configure the operating system. Often, hardware and software configurations need to be investigated as prerequisites to adding a new application or piece of hardware.

This chapter will introduce some of the basic commands used to investigate the configuration of a Linux server. We will also look into some commands used to evaluate the status of the system.

It may also be necessary to determine the effects of adding new hardware or software to the server. Some examples of questions that might arise are:

- What are the top resource consumers on the system?

- Is the system I/O bound or CPU bound?

- How did adding disk and distributing the data affect I/O throughput?

- Did adding memory to the system improve memory performance?

First let's look at how to view the processor information in a Linux box.

CPU Related Information

Linux keeps information regarding the processor(s) in a server in a file called **/proc/cpuinfo**. The following are sample contents of the **/proc/cpuinfo** file from a basic Linux system:

```
# cat /proc/cpuinfo

processor       : 0
vendor_id       : GenuineIntel
cpu family      : 6
model           : 5
model name      : Pentium II (Deschutes)
stepping        : 1
cpu MHz         : 398.273
cache size      : 512 KB
fdiv_bug        : no
hlt_bug         : no
f00f_bug        : no
coma_bug        : no
fpu             : yes
fpu_exception   : yes
cpuid level     : 2
wp              : yes
flags           : fpu vme de pse tsc msr pae mce cx8 apic sep mtrr
pge mca cmov pat pse36 mmx fxsr
bogomips        : 794.62
```

The important information here is the vendor, model, CPU speed in MHz and cache size of this processor. These are the factors most likely to affect performance. Other information, like whether the processor is susceptible to some known CPU-related bugs, and whether it has a floating point unit (fpu) may also be useful, but have less effect on overall performance. The bogomips reference is an ambiguous speed rating calculated during boot-up. If the server contained multiple processors, the information in this listing would be repeated for each processor.

Display the Number of Processors in the Server

If we want to know how many processors a system has we can just look to see how many individual entries there are in the **/proc/cpuinfo** file. If we wanted an easier way to check the number of processes we can use **grep** and **wc** to check the file for us like this:

```
# cat /proc/cpuinfo | grep processor | wc -l
1
```

Here we have output the **/proc/cpuinfo** file with the **cat** command then used **grep** to eliminate all lines from the output which do not contain the string **'processor'**. We then use **wc −l** to count the number of lines left in the output. The count is 1 so we know this system only has one processor.

Displaying the Total RAM on the Linux system

Linux stores memory related information in a file called **/proc/meminfo**. The **meminfo** file can be listed to see the current state of system memory:

```
# cat /proc/meminfo
MemTotal:        257124 kB
MemFree:          67388 kB
Buffers:          20516 kB
Cached:          124140 kB
SwapCached:           0 kB
Active:           51736 kB
Inactive:        108328 kB
HighTotal:            0 kB
HighFree:             0 kB
LowTotal:        257124 kB
LowFree:          67388 kB
SwapTotal:       524152 kB
SwapFree:        524152 kB
Dirty:                0 kB
Writeback:            0 kB
Mapped:           27752 kB
Slab:             26424 kB
Committed_AS:     64300 kB
PageTables:        1044 kB
VmallocTotal:   3874808 kB
VmallocUsed:       1260 kB
VmallocChunk:   3873360 kB
HugePages_Total:      0
HugePages_Free:       0
```

Some of the key points to this output are the MemTotal which is the total amount of memory in the system and the MemFree which shows how much unused memory is available. The SwapTotal and SwapFree lines represent the same information but for swap (disk currently being used as memory.)

The Linux **free** command extracts and formats pertinent information from the **meminfo**. While not as detailed **free** displays some big-picture information about the system:

```
# free -k
              total       used       free     shared    buffers     cached
Mem:         257124     189736      67388          0      20572     124140
-/+ buffers/cache:       45024     212100
Swap:        524152          0     524152
```

Some information in the above display is extracted directly from the **meminfo** file while other information is calculated. The display shows how much memory is being used in kilobytes, because the **-k** option has been specified. If you prefer to see the information in megabytes you can use the **–m** option.

Top Memory and CPU Users

Previously, the process status (**ps**) command was introduced. When the **-u** option is specified with the **ps** command, columns representing the percentage of CPU and the percentage of memory that a process is using are displayed as represented below by columns *%cpu* and *%mem*.

```
# ps u
USER        PID %CPU %MEM   VSZ  RSS TTY      STAT START    TIME
COMMAND
terry      4968  0.0  0.5  5644 1320 pts/6    S    11:21   0:00 -bash
terry      5120  0.0  0.2  3440  756 pts/6    R    11:42   0:00 ps u
```

The **aux** options can be added to the **ps** command to include all processes, not just the user's own and build a complex command to display the commands using the most memory or CPU.

An example of each complex command is included below:

Display Top CPU User:

```
# ps -aux | sort -n +2 | tail -1
root      2201  0.2  3.2 36564 8464 ?         S    Oct17   2:18
/usr/X11R6/bin/X :0 -audit 0 -auth /var/gdm/:0.Xauth -nolisten tcp
vt7
```

Display Top Memory User:

```
# ps -aux | sort -n +3 | tail -1
gdm       3718  0.0  3.5 20744 9012 ?         S    00:09   0:36
/usr/bin/gdmgreeter
```

In the example above that can be used for displaying the top memory user, all processes are displayed then sorted in ascending sequence using the numeric value found in column 4 (**sort** defaults to the first column and the **+3** tells **sort** to look three columns to the right of that.) It then displays the last and highest value in the sorted list. If you wanted to see the top five memory or CPU users we could just change the **tail -1** to **tail -5**, just remember they will be sorted from least to greatest of the top 5. We'll talk more about building complex commands like this in the chapter on shell scripting.

Paging and Swapping Devices

Linux uses a swap disk as a repository for segments of memory that are paged out from physical RAM. Linux will use swap very intelligently even when sufficient physical memory is available. When too many things are running at once and the demand for memory exceeds the size of physical memory excessive paging will likely take place, eventually impacting system performance. The Linux default is to set the size of the swap disk to twice the size of physical RAM installed in the server.

Linux stores information about devices used for system paging and swapping activities in a file called **/proc/swaps**. To display information regarding swap devices, the file can be displayed using

either the **cat** command or the **swapon** command with the **-s** option.
As shown below, the results are the same using either method.

```
# cat /proc/swaps
Filename              Type        Size      Used   Priority
/dev/hdf2             partition   524152    0      -1
# swapon -s
Filename              Type        Size      Used   Priority
/dev/hdf2             partition   524152    0      -1
```

Here we see the device name, type, size and amount used for each
swap device. In this case we only have the one swap device.

Kernel Parameters

Linux is a parameter driven system. Kernel parameters used for system
configuration are found in **/proc/sys/kernel**, where there is an
individual file for each configuration parameter. Since these parameters
have a direct effect on system performance, root access is required in
order to modify them.

You can view the current configuration parameters by using the **cat**
command on the appropriate file.

```
# cat msgmax
8192
```

Occasionally, a prerequisite to a software installation requires the
modification of kernel parameters. Since each parameter file contains
a single line of data consisting of either a text string or numeric values,
it is often easy to modify a parameter by simply using the **echo**
command:

```
# echo 2048 > /proc/sys/kernel/msgmax
```

The aforementioned command will set the value of the *msgmax*
parameter to 2048. This change will only remain in effect until the
system is rebooted.

Linux also provides the **sysctl** command to modify kernel parameters at runtime. **sysctl** uses parameter information stored in a file called **/etc/sysctl.conf**. If, for example, we needed to change the value of the *msgmax* parameter as was accomplished above, we could accomplish the same thing with the **sysctl** command like this:

```
# sysctl -w kernel.msgmax=2048
```

The next section will introduce some useful utilities that are provided with most Linux releases. These utilities allow some interactive monitoring of the system.

Server monitoring commands

Some popular commands/utilities for monitoring system resources and tasks managed by the Linux kernel are as follows:

- **top:** Provides a dynamic real-time view of a running system, including information about system resource usage and a constantly updated list of the processes which are consuming the most resources. Because it is so useful for administration we will talk quite a bit about **top** in chapter 8.

- **mpstat**: Reports activities for each available processor, processor zero being the first one reported. Global average activities across all processors are also reported.

- **iostat:** Used for monitoring the load on system input/output devices by observing the time the devices are active compared to the average transfer rate of the device.

- **vmstat**: Displays information about processes, memory, paging, block IO, and different levels of CPU activity

Interactive Statistics using the top Utility

The **top** program provides a dynamic real-time view of a running Linux system. This can be one of the most useful ways to monitor the system as it shows several key statistics on the same page with

---

information on the busiest processes. It is also one of the few commands which will constantly update. For more information on the **top** utility refer to chapter 8.

Displaying Multi-Processor Statistics

The **mpstat** command displays statistics for each and every processor within the system. The **mpstat** command accepts *interval* (delay) and *count* (repeat) values as parameters. **mpstat** will repeat the output *count* times every *interval* seconds. This is very useful for monitoring changes over time.

The following example uses an *interval* of three seconds and a *count* of five iterations of the report detail lines. An average summary line is produced at the end of the report.

```
$ mpstat 3 5
Linux 2.6.5-1.358 (Dell-Linux)  10/18/2004
10:33:26 PM  CPU   %user  %nice %system %iowait   %irq   %soft  %idle   intr/s
10:33:29 PM  all    1.00   0.00    0.33    0.00    0.00    0.00  98.67  1001.99
10:33:32 PM  all    0.33   0.00    0.33    0.00    0.00    0.00  99.33  1007.02
10:33:35 PM  all    0.67   0.00    0.33    0.00    0.00    0.00  99.00  1002.67
10:33:38 PM  all    0.66   0.00    0.33    0.00    0.00    0.00  99.00  1000.33
10:33:41 PM  all    0.67   0.00    0.33    0.00    0.00    0.00  99.00  1005.67
Average:     all    0.67   0.00    0.33    0.00    0.00    0.00  99.00  1003.53
```

The columns in the report generated by the **mpstat** command are defined as follows:

- CPU: Either the processor number or the keyword *all*, which indicates that statistics are calculated as averages among all processors or that there is only one processor in the server

- *%user*: The percentage of CPU used by user applications

- *%nice*: The percentage of CPU utilization at the user level with nice priority

- *%system*: The percentage of CPU used by the system. This does not include the time spent servicing interrupts or softirqs. A softirq is a software interrupt, one of up to 32 software interrupts which can run on multiple CPUs simultaneously.

- *%iowait*: The percentage of time the system had a pending disk I/O request

- *%irq*: The percentage of time spent by the CPUs servicing interrupts

- *%soft*: The percentage of time the processors spent servicing softirqs.

- *%idle*: The percentage of time that the processors were idle and the system did not have a pending disk I/O request.

- *intr/s*: The total number of interrupts per second received by the processor(s)

The information from the **mpstat** report can be used to determine if processor load is being distributed evenly across the existing processors and if the multi-processing capabilities of the server are being utilized effectively.

Displaying I/O Statistics

The **iostat** command is used to monitor the load on server input/output (I/O) devices by observing the time the devices are active compared to the average transfer rate of the device. **iostat** generates several report lines that can be used to monitor and subsequently change the system configuration to better balance the I/O workload between physical disk devices.

The initial report detail lines generated by **iostat** provide statistics encompassing the time since the system was last booted. Subsequent sets of detail lines cover the time since the previous report interval.

Each set of report lines starts with a header row with CPU statistics which represents the CPU usage across all processors. Following the CPU information, a device header row is displayed with subsequent detail lines of statistics for each device in the system.

The following example shows the invocation of **iostat** specifying a three second interval or delay with a total of five samplings or counts:

```
$ iostat 3 5
Linux 2.6.5-1.358 (Dell-Linux)  10/18/2004
```

```
avg-cpu:  %user    %nice    %sys %iowait    %idle
           0.51     0.14    0.22    0.26    98.86

Device:            tps   Blk_read/s   Blk_wrtn/s   Blk_read   Blk_wrtn
hda               0.00         0.02         0.00       1192         38
hdf               0.99        20.83         5.33    1405186     359616

avg-cpu:  %user    %nice    %sys %iowait    %idle
           0.67     0.00    0.33    0.00    99.00

Device:            tps   Blk_read/s   Blk_wrtn/s   Blk_read   Blk_wrtn
hda               0.00         0.00         0.00          0          0
hdf               0.00         0.00         0.00          0          0

avg-cpu:  %user    %nice    %sys %iowait    %idle
           0.67     0.00    0.33    0.00    99.00

Device:            tps   Blk_read/s   Blk_wrtn/s   Blk_read   Blk_wrtn
hda               0.00         0.00         0.00          0          0
```

For the average CPU report, *%user*, *%nice*, *%iowait*, and *%idle* are defined the same as they were in the *mpstat* command output. One remaining piece of information is defined as:

- *%sys*: The percentage of processor utilization occurring at the system kernel level.

For the device utilization report:

- *device*: The device name as listed in the /dev directory is displayed. These device names are mapped to mount points in the file /etc/fstab and are also listed in the output of the **df** command.

- *tps*: The number of transfers (I/O requests) per second issued to the device.

- *blk_read/s*: The number of blocks per second read from the device.

- *blk_wrtn/s*: The number of blocks per second written to the device.

- *blk_read*: The total number of blocks read.

- *blk_wrtn*: The total number of blocks written.

This information can assist in the determination of which devices are more heavily used than others and perhaps help with the determination of how to better distribute data to balance the workload.

Displaying Virtual Memory Statistics

The **vmstat** command displays information about processes, memory, paging, block IO, and different levels of CPU activity. As with **iostat**, the first detail lines produce report averages since the last reboot. Subsequent detail lines report information using the interval specified on the command line.

As with the other commands in this section, the **vmstat** command is driven by delay and count options that determine the time interval between report lines and the totals number of intervals to be reported.

```
$ vmstat 3 5
procs -----------memory---------- ---swap-- -----io---- --system-- ----cpu----
 r  b   swpd   free   buff  cache   si   so    bi    bo   in   cs us sy id wa
 0  0      0  63492  94856  24996    0    0     8     3  484   29  1  0 99  0
 0  0      0  63492  94856  24996    0    0     0     0 1005   25  1  0 99  0
 0  0      0  63492  94860  24996    0    0     0    13 1005   24  1  0 99  0
 0  0      0  63492  94860  24996    0    0     0     0 1002   21  0  0 99  0
 0  0      0  63492  94864  24996    0    0     0     4 1003   22  1  0 99  0
```

The Linux man page for **vmstat** defines the fields displayed as follows:

- *procs*

    - *r*: The number of processes waiting for run time

    - *b*: The number of processes in uninterruptible sleep, which means they are waiting on a resource

- *memory*

    - *swpd*: Virtual memory used

    - *free*: Idle memory

    - *buff*: Amount of memory used as buffers

    - *cache*: Current memory used as cache

- *swap*

    - *si*: Memory swapped in per second from disk

    - *so*: Memory swapped out per second to disk

- *io*

Easy Linux Commands

- *bi*: Blocks per second received from a block device
- *bo*: Blocks per second sent to a block device
- *system*
  - *in*:.Number of interrupts per second, including the clock
  - *cs*: Number of context switches per second
- *cpu*: These statistics are percentages of total CPU time:
  - *us*: User time spent running non-kernel code, includes nice time
  - *sy*: System time spent running kernel code
  - *id*: Idle time
  - *wa*: Wait time spent waiting for I/O

The **vmstat** information can be invaluable when studying resource utilization trends. Here are a few examples of how **vmstat** output can be interpreted:

If over time the run queue value, *procs-r*, remains consistently higher than the number of processors in the server and CPU idle time is low, the system is CPU bound and can benefit from the addition of more and/or faster processors. Alternatively a high number displayed in the *procs-b* column also indicates a bottleneck, but one where processes are waiting on other resources.

If the virtual memory used (*memory-swpd*) remains high and the free memory (*memory-free*) remains low, then the system is memory constrained and will benefit from additional RAM.

Consistently high I/O rates paired with consistently low CPU utilization (*cpu-us*) indicates an I/O bound system that could benefit from a highly buffered disk array or possibly solid-state disk.

Conclusions

In this chapter we started off with some commands which can be used to examine the configuration of a Linux box. This is often useful if you are using a system which has been configured by someone else or when you need to check the configuration of a system without the luxury of shutting it down and cracking the case.

We then learned how to search the system for processes with certain statistics by combining the **ps** and **sort** commands. We also briefly went over how to examine the system for memory paging and swapping and how to set many kernel parameters which may need to be customized before installing software.

Perhaps the most valuable portion of this chapter covered the use of **top**, **mpstat**, **iostat** and **vmstat** to obtain a myriad of statistics about the system. Tons of information directly pertaining to system performance can be obtained from the output of these utilities and most of them have the ability to report statistics since system startup and over a specified period of time.

In the next couple chapters we will take a step back from examining and monitoring the system and talk about how to set up and maintain a filesystem.

Disk and Filesystem Commands

In this chapter we'll handle some basic methods for examining and disks and partitions in Linux. These commands need to be used carefully as it would be easy to accidentally erase data, and that's never good!

Before we talk too much about partitions and mount points it is important to understand that a Linux mount point can be anywhere you could put a directory. While at the base of any Linux system there is a **/** directory, commonly called the *root* directory a partition may be mounted anywhere below that. Here are some examples of common mount points and what you might find there:

Mount Point	Contents
/	the slash partition is where everything starts
/boot	contains essential boot files
/usr/local	reserved for installed software 'local' to this computer
/tmp	temporary files for this system or any applications on it

Here we see that */usr/local* is listed as a partition; however, it does not come directly below the root (/) partition. This takes a little getting used to, but just be aware that a disk partition can be mounted anywhere.

Displaying File System Information

It is very common to have to examine disk use to determine where there is free space, where the disk may be nearing full and where you may need to add disk or move files. One of the most essential commands used to examine disks is the **df** command.

The **df** command is used to display information about mounted file systems. By default the **df** command will typically return disk information in kilobytes. Since there can be variation on this default behavior it is often nice to use the **–k** option which will force **df** to displays disk space usage in kilobytes as seen in this example:

```
$ df -k
Filesystem           1K-blocks       Used Available Use% Mounted on
/dev/hdf1            18727836     2595832  15180656  15% /
/dev/hda1              101086        5945     89922   7% /boot
none                  128560           0    128560   0% /dev/shm
```

These results show that two file systems are mounted. The *Filesystem* column of the output shows the path to the disk device which is currently mounted at the *Mounted on* location. The *1K-blocks* column displays the size of the entire partition while the *Used* and *Available* columns indicate the number of 1K blocks on that device used and available. The *Use%* column will show what percentage of the disk is currently used and is the quickest way to identify disks which are getting full.

To get the display in a friendlier format, the **–h** option can be used:

```
$ df -h
Filesystem           Size  Used Avail Use% Mounted on
/dev/hdf1             18G   2.5G   15G  15% /
/dev/hda1             99M   5.9M   88M   7% /boot
none                 126M      0  126M   0% /dev/shm
```

The **-h** option will show output in the familiar gigabyte, megabyte or kilobyte (*G*, *M* or *K* respectively) scales. This makes things more human readable, hence the *h*.

It is easy to see that the first file system is 18GB in size, with 2.5GB used and 15GB of available free space. It is mounted on the root (/) mount point.

The second file system is 99MB in size, with 5.9MB used and 88MB of available free space. It is mounted on the */boot* mount point.

This output also shows a shared memory space of 126MB currently available (*/dev/shm*).

Creating a File System

Some file systems are created automatically during the Linux installation process. For instance, when I set up a system with Fedora Core 2 (Red Hat) for this book, the installation tool detected the two disk drives and offered to automatically configure their partitions and setup a file system.

There are many different types of file systems. Microsoft Windows administrators are familiar with filesystems like FAT16, FAT32, and NTFS. The comparable options on Linux are ext2, ext3, and Linux-swap. The differences between these filesystem types are beyond the scope of this book.

During the lifetime of a Linux system it is not uncommon to want to add additional disk space to a system by adding disks or replace a current drive with a larger capacity. Here are some of the most useful commands for setting up disks:

Note: You will need root privileges to perform most of these tasks.

Command	Function
fdisk	Partition a hard disk
fsck	Check and optionally repair one or more Linux file systems
mkdir	Make a new file directory
mkfs	Make a file system
mkswap	Make a swap area on a device or in a file
mount	Mount a file system (umount to unmount)
parted	Disk partitioning and partition resizing program. It allows the user to create, destroy, resize, move and copy ext2, ext3, Linux-swap, FAT and FAT32 partitions.
sfdisk	List the size of a partition, the partitions on a device, check the partitions on a device, and repartition a device.

Table 3.1: *Commands for file system creation*

Installing a disk

While the exact steps will be vendor specific (always consult the documentation for your hardware and software) here is the overall procedure for installing a new disk in a typical desktop Linux workstation. In the example described below we are adding a new drive to an open drive bay.

Here is a quick overview of the steps we will take to setup a new disk:

1. Shut down the system

2. Install the drive into an open drive bay

3. Startup the system and enter the BIOS to make the hardware aware of the new disk

4. Partition the new disk with **fdisk**

5. Format the new partition with **mkfs**

6. Mount the new partition with the **mount** command

7. Add the new partition to the **/etc/fstab** file so it will be mounted at startup time in the future

Most workstations have IDE or EIDE hard drives. SATA has also recently become a popular option. Modern onboard EIDE controllers can handle four attached devices. Typically at least one of these devices is a CD-ROM or DVD-ROM drive and one other is a hard drive. In Linux, these four devices are identified as *hda, hdb, hdc,* and *hdd* in the */dev* directory. The hard disks can have many partitions on each disk and the partitions are also identified in the */dev* directory. For example, */dev/hda2* refers to the second partition on the hard disk connected to the first controller port.

Follow your manufacturer's instructions and any instructions that came with the hard drive to install the drive in a free bay. I would give you more specific instructions here if I could, but the methods for the hardware part of installing and configuring a drive vary widely between manufacturers. Especially close attention must be paid to jumper settings on the hard drives.

If there are no free bays or ports left you may need to replace one of the installed drives, just be careful you don't remove the drive you're booting from. It is important to remember to hook up both the IDE and power cables before closing the machine; otherwise you will be very disappointed with the results.

As the machine boots you will want to enter the BIOS setup for the system to make the hardware aware of the new disks presence. The methods of entering the BIOS also vary from machine to machine but most systems will tell you just as they start booting up how to enter the BIOS.

Partition the New Disk

Now that we've installed the disk and we know its device path we are ready to partition it. The **fdisk** command is used to set up Linux partitions. Older versions of Microsoft Windows had a utility called **fdisk** which shared both name and function with the Linux version, but the Linux one is a bit different so be careful.

 Make sure you get the right disk here! If you repartition a disk with **fdisk** all data on affected partitions will be lost!

We invoke the **fdisk** command with the device path to the disk we want to partition:

```
fdisk /dev/hdb
The number of cylinders for this disk is set to 1401.
There is nothing wrong with that, but this is larger than 1024,
and could in certain setups cause problems with:
1) software that runs at boot time (e.g., old versions of LILO)
2) booting and partitioning software from other OSs
   (e.g., DOS FDISK, OS/2 FDISK)

Command (m for help): m
Command action
   a   toggle a bootable flag
```

```
    b   edit bsd disklabel
    c   toggle the dos compatibility flag
    d   delete a partition
    l   list known partition types
    m   print this menu
    n   add a new partition
    o   create a new empty DOS partition table
    p   print the partition table
    q   quit without saving changes
    s   create a new empty Sun disklabel
    t   change a partition's system id
    u   change display/entry units
    v   verify the partition table
    w   write table to disk and exit
    x   extra functionality (experts only)

Command (m for help): p

Disk /dev/hda: 11.5 GB, 11525455872 bytes
255 heads, 63 sectors/track, 1401 cylinders
Units = cylinders of 16065 * 512 = 8225280 bytes

   Device Boot      Start         End      Blocks   Id  System

Command (m for help):
```

The *fdisk* utility is menu driven. The **m** command can be used to show the menu options available at the main menu. Also shown above, the **p** command will print the partition layout currently on that disk.

```
Command (m for help): n
Command action
   e   extended
   p   primary partition (1-4)
p
Partition number (1-4): 1
First cylinder (14-9726, default 14):
Using default value 1
Last cylinder or +size or +sizeM or +sizeK (1-9726, default 9726):
Using default value 9726

Command (m for help): w
```

The **n** menu selection can be used to create a new partition. You can then choose to create it as an extended (**e**) or primary (**p**) partition type. Typically you will want to create a primary partition. Next select a partition number. On a new disk **1** should be appropriate. We can then type **w** to write out the new partition table to the disk and it will be ready to format.

Easy Linux Commands

Format the New Disk

Next, the **mkfs** (make file system) commands would be used to format Linux partitions using an *ext3* file system on the new partition. Now when we are referring to the device path we also include the partition number (in this case **1**) that we just created.

```
$ mkfs -t ext3 -c /dev/hdb1
```

The **−t** option is used to specify the type of filesystem to create. The **−c** option specified here will cause **mkfs** to check the partition for bad blocks (physical defects in the disk) before creating the file system.

If you want to format a swap partition on the new disk, the **mkswap** command can be used instead of **mkfs** as follows:

```
$ mkswap -c /dev/hdb1
```

Notice that we do not have to specify the partition type since **mkswap** will only create swap partitions. The **−c** option can still be used to check for bad blocks.

Mount the New Disk

The next step is to create a directory for use as a mount point for our new partition. The **mkdir** command is used to create a directory, in this case called **/new1**. There is nothing special about this directory but it's best to keep it empty since any contents of this directory will disappear when the new partition is mounted at that location.

```
$ mkdir /new1
```

Now that we have created our mount point we can mount the partition making it available for use:

```
$ mount -t ext3 /dev/hdb1 /new1
```

Here we see that the **mount** command takes several options. First the **-t ext3** specifies the partition type, the same type which was used for the newfs command. The next option, **/dev/hdb1**, specifies the device path and the final option listed here, **/new1** is the mount point we just created.

We could now start using the new disk at the location **/new1** but when the system reboots the **/new1** partition will not be mounted! To make it mount automatically we will need to add it to the **/etc/fstab** file.

Working with the File System Table

When adding a disk or changing disk layout it is necessary to modify the file system table. The table is found in a file called **/etc/fstab**. The following listing contains the contents of **fstab** on the test server at this point:

```
$ cat /etc/fstab
LABEL=/                 /                    ext3    defaults        1 1
LABEL=/boot             /boot                ext3    defaults        1 2
none                    /dev/pts             devpts  gid=5,mode=620  0 0
none                    /dev/shm             tmpfs   defaults        0 0
none                    /proc                proc    defaults        0 0
none                    /sys                 sysfs   defaults        0 0
/dev/hdf2               swap                 swap    defaults        0 0
/dev/cdrom              /mnt/cdrom           udf,iso9660 noauto,owner,kudzu,ro 0 0
/dev/cdrom1             /mnt/cdrom1          udf,iso9660 noauto,owner,kudzu,ro 0 0
/dev/hdc4               /mnt/zip             auto    noauto,owner,kudzu 0 0
/dev/fd0                /mnt/floppy          auto    noauto,owner,kudzu 0 0
```

Each line in the *fstab* file consists of six fields separated by spaces or tabs.

The contents of the fields are described in Table 3.2, as follows:

Field	Description
1	The physical device or remote file system being described
2	The mount point where the file system will be mounted
3	The type of file system on this device
4	A list of options which mount uses when mounting the file system.
5	This field is used by the dump backup utility to determine if a file system should be backed up. If this field is zero, the dump will ignore that file system.
6	This field is used by the **fsck** file system check utility to determine the order in which file systems should be checked. If the field is zero, **fsck** will not check this file system.

Table 3.2: *fstab file fields*

The */etc/fstab* file can be modified to change what devices will be mounted where or, in our case, to make a new device mount at boot. Using a text editor (like **vi** which covered in chapter 5) we can *carefully* add the following line to the **/etc/fstab** file to make new1 mount at boot:

```
/dev/hdb1          /new1          ext3    defaults       1 1
```

Our **/new1** partition will now be available every time we reboot the system! Be careful to double and triple check any changes to the **/etc/fstab** file before rebooting the system.

LVM: The Logical Volume Manager

While the management of hard disk volumes is an advanced topic and will not be presented in detail in this guide, the Logical Volume Manager (LVM) subsystem provided in Linux for Systems Administrators is worthy of mention. It can be used to create and manage disk volume groups from physical disk volumes. By allowing physically separate disks to be combined into a single logical disk, LVM simplifies many aspects of disk management. When working from a simple Linux workstation with one or two internal disk drives, there will likely be no need to use LVM; however when administrating

Linux servers that have arrays of disks attached LVM can be invaluable.

The user must have root access in order to use the LVM subsystem. LVM is a parameter driven subsystem controlled by specifications found in the text file located at **/etc/lvm/lvm.conf.** The configuration file contains several comments which describe each section. The LVM subsystem has over 40 commands for the creation and management of volume groups. Though this book does not cover LVM, table 3.3 below contains a partial list of available LVM subcommands to give you a taste of what LVM is capable of:

Subcommand	Function
lvchange	Change attributes of a logical volume
lvcreate	Create a logical volume in an existing volume group
lvdisplay	Display attributes of a logical volume
lvextend	Add space to a logical volume
lvmdiskscan	List devices that may be used as physical volumes
lvreduce	Reduce the size of a logical volume
lvresize	Resize a logical volume
vgcreate	Create a volume group
vgdisplay	Display volume group information
vgextend	Add physical volumes to a volume group

Table 3.3: *LVM subcommands and their functions*

It is clear that LVM is a rather sophisticated subsystem, and users definitely need to know what they are doing and be very careful when using it; otherwise, it would be easy to clobber the disk configuration and render the system unusable.

Conclusions

In this chapter we learned a little about how Linux organizes its disks and how we can examine what disks are currently available within a system with the **df** command.

After a quick overview of the commands used for filesystem manipulation we then stepped through the setup of a filesystem.

Starting with the physical installation of a new hard drive, then partitioning, formatting, mounting and finally setup of the **/etc/fstab** file to make the partition mount when the system is rebooted.

The Logical Volume Manager (**LVM**) subsystem was included as well as some of the commands it supports for creating and managing resources such as disk arrays.

Book Summary

This concludes the Linux Quick Reference. While no book can make you an expert we hope that this one has eased the learning curve and will continue to act as a functional reference.

If you're interested increasing your Linux expertise the best way to do it is experience. The more you use Linux the better you'll get at it, especially if you work a lot at the command line!

Linux skills are always desirable in the IT field and many of your Linux skills will carry over to UNIX and other UNIX-like operating systems, even Mac OSX! The ability to operate at the command line not only allows you to work things out when your windowing environment will not start but also can allow you to connect remotely from anywhere in the world via SSH.

If you want to learn more about Linux shell scripting check out *Oracle Shell Scripting: Linux and UNIX Programming for Oracle* by Jon Emmons. Though some of this book is geared specifically toward Oracle professionals much of it can be applied on any Linux or UNIX system.

About Jon Emmons

 Jon Emmons has been designing and deploying Linux and UNIX systems for several years. With experience in both corporate and higher education Jon has managed implementations ranging from desktop workstations for academic research to large multi-tier load balanced custom web application farms.

Shortly after college, Jon's command of system administration identified him as a good candidate for database administration. Since then he has been working extensively with Oracle database and application server on UNIX and Linux.

Jon has been publishing about system and database administration on his blog, **www.LifeAfterCoffe.com** since 2005. Jon often answers technical questions submitted to his blog by readers and also authored the popular Caffeine WordPress theme (available at www.lifeaftercoffee.com/caffeine/), a theme which is designed specifically to be easy to customize. Jon's blog continues to receive acclaim from the online community.

In addition to his technical abilities Jon has also been called upon to teach a college course in database management systems.

Originally from Maine, Jon now lives in Concord, NH and enjoys kayaking, skiing, hunting, flying radio controlled model airplanes, playing guitar and cooking.

About Terry Clark

Terry Clark is an Oracle Certified DBA with more than 25 years of full-time IT experience.

Certified in client-server and LAN technologies by DePaul University, Terry has extensive experience with Linux troubleshooting and tuning database networks.

An acknowledge Linux and Oracle expert, Terry has published in Oracle Internals Magazine and has over a decade of Oracle experience working with mission-critical Linux and UNIX systems. Terry specializes in Linux Oracle tuning and troubleshooting and is noted for his ability to quickly identify and correct production problems. Terry lives in Las Vegas where he enjoys Toastmasters and Real Estate speculation.

About Mike Reed

When he first started drawing, Mike Reed drew just to amuse himself. It wasn't long, though, before he knew he wanted to be an artist. Today he does illustrations for children's books, magazines, catalogs, and ads.

He also teaches illustration at the College of Visual Art in St. Paul, Minnesota. Mike Reed says, "Making pictures is like acting — you can paint yourself into the action." He often paints on the computer, but he also draws in pen and ink and paints in acrylics. He feels that learning to draw well is the key to being a successful artist.

Mike is regarded as one of the nation's premier illustrators and is the creator of the popular "Flame Warriors" illustrations at **www.flamewarriors.com**, a website devoted to Internet insults. "To enter his Flame Warriors site is sort of like entering a hellish Sesame Street populated by Oscar the Grouch and 83 of his relatives." – Los Angeles Times.
(http://redwing.hutman.net/%7Emreed/warriorshtm/lat.htm)

Mike Reed has always enjoyed reading. As a young child, he liked the Dr. Seuss books. Later, he started reading biographies and war stories. One reason why he feels lucky to be an illustrator is because he can listen to books on tape while he works. Mike is available to provide custom illustrations for all manner of publications at reasonable prices. Mike can be reached at **www.mikereedillustration.com**.

Index

Get the Easy Oracle Series

Oracle is the world's most complex and robust database, and it takes special skill to get you started in Oracle the easy way. These books are designed by certified Oracle experts and trainers who have years of experience explaining complex Oracle topics in plain English.

- **Easy Oracle Jumpstart** – Get started fast with Oracle.

- **Easy Oracle SQL and SQL*Plus** – Get started fast writing Oracle queries.

- **Easy Oracle PL/SQL Programming** – A proven step-by-step approach to programming with Oracle PL/SQL.

- **Easy Oracle Automation** – Learn about the automation features of Oracle.

- **Easy Oracle PHP** – Learn how to create powerful web applications using the Oracle database.

- **Free Oracle 10g Reference Poster** – Just Google "free Oracle poster" to get your free copy of the Oracle reference poster.

These books are priced right to help you get started fast in Oracle technology.

www.rampant.cc

Oracle 10g Senior DBA Reference Poster

This 24 x 36 inch quick reference includes the important data columns and relationships between the DBA views, allowing you to quickly write complex data dictionary queries.

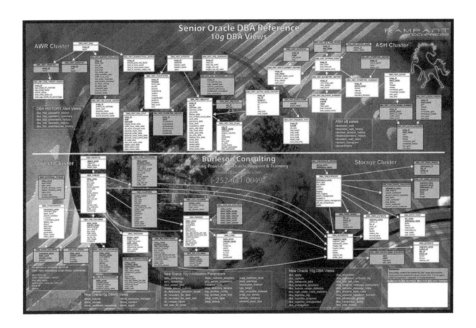

This comprehensive data dictionary reference contains the most important columns from the most important Oracle10g DBA views. Especially useful are the Automated Workload Repository (AWR) and Active Session History (ASH) DBA views.

WARNING - This poster is not suitable for beginners. It is designed for senior Oracle DBAs and requires knowledge of Oracle data dictionary internal structures. You can get your poster at this URL:

www.rampant.cc/poster.htm